World Of Wet

Selected Poems By

Edward L. Smith
&
Carmen M. Pursifull

A Hawk Production.

This is a Hawk Production

Carmen M. Pursifull
Hawk Productions
809 West Maple Street
Champaign, Illinois 61820-2810

Library Of Congress Control Number: 2002109075

ISBN# 1-881900-12-6

First Edition 2002

Edited by Marie Mamaril

Cover:
Original painting by Edward L. Smith.
Graphics by Steven Kappes.

Back cover:
Steven Kappes.

Printed in the United States Of America.

Typeset by Carmen M. Pursifull

Editor's Introduction

Poets such as Carmen M. Pursifull and Edward L. Smith are unique guardians of imagination, the lyric voice expressing its encounter with the puzzling, but awesome universe. In the poetry selection of *World of Wet*, Smith and Pursifull combine their poetic expressiveness to create a humanizing force in our world of uncertainty, which often imprisons our imagination, capturing it in passivity without humane content. This selection of poems not only stimulate my imagination, as well as its readers, it also provides an opportunity for all its readers to explore human values. The candor in The World of Wet is startling -- and refreshing. As the editor of this collection of selected poetry, I welcome this new openness. Dr. Edward Smith and Ms. Pursifull do not avoid sensitive subjects that might not play well with readers such as death, serious concerns for environmental issues, aging, lost relationships and the September 11th attacks.

There is nothing conventional about the poetry found in *World of Wet*. Although Smith and Pursifull have vastly different life experiences and different writing styles, they collaborated masterly to write in a fluid and graceful manner which speaks in soothing measured tones of a spiritual leader stretching the reader's imagination beyond reality. Dr. Smith writes in a subtle, reserved manner, but with unblinking honesty and knowledge and Ms. Pursifull's style is frank and tends to spring her readers into action. It is their combined talents which makes this collection unique with its realistic sensuality and some times shocking and emotional tones. Some poems are raw and caustic, while some border the subtle shades of gray in a reader's interpretation. Other poems are playful in mood such as in "Diving For Calamari" or "My Taxes Waxes."

The collection is gutsy and deserves credit for recognizing thorny issues. Many of the poems' imageries compete with popular representations such as in the section, "The Intruders." In this section, the poems exemplify the myriad of emotions, beliefs, desires, questions, and doubts of people who deal with health issues either directly or indirectly. Even though our concerns are seemingly trivial at times, they do become important at some point of our lives. Such emotions are common in our lives every day. These poems are truly exceptional and insightful because words of hope prevail through faith and love.

When I read the poems, "Yesterday" and "Impedimenta," I experience vividly the fear and pain over the terrorist attacks and sympathy with its victims as most readers. Ms. Pursifull and Dr. Smith understand their audience and communicate effectively in this collection of poems what we take either for granted or are too afraid to consider.

Edward and Carmen do not hide the truth about their passions, their curiosity about the universe, or their strong faith even when faced with harrowing experiences that no one would ever want to undergo. I find their poetry humbling because I cannot escape from being intrusive. Pursifull and Smith find the courage to make themselves vulnerable; to revisit emotions and traumas in these works that ordinary people would shun. They speak the unspeakable in the World of Wet from the breathtaking beauty of "Remembering Tomorrow" to the brutality of life which leaves its readers an aftertaste that is like exquisite champagne.

Marie Mamaril,
Editor

Bio of Marie Mamaril.

Marie Mamaril has essays and poetry in publications such as Pacific Enterprise, The Philippine News, Dream International Quarterly, and Matrix. She is a member of The Red Herring Poets and Skyland Writers and Artists Association. She holds a MAT from Fairleigh Dickinson University. Her works include Expressions of Life, A Gift of Gratitude, and Return to Innocence. Ms. Mamaril is a writer, poet, instructor of English, and freelance editor. She lives in Illinois.

Other Works by the Authors.

Edward L. Smith.

Motion In The Ocean: Tides, Waves, And Currents. Academic Press, New York, New York. (1967)

The Propagation Of Underwater Sound In Antisubmarine Warfare. United States Government Printing Office, Washington, D.C. (1969)

Signal Processing Of Underwater Sound. with C. W. Thornton. United States Government Printing Office, Washington, D.C. (1979)

The Kuroshio: The Japan Current. Technical Editor. Symposium Proceedings. East-West Center, University of Hawaii. (1974). Sponsored by United Nations Educational, Scientific, and Cultural Organization. UNESCO.

Carmen M. Pursifull.

Carmen By Moonlight. Poetry. (1982)

The Twenty-Four Hour Wake. Poetry. (1989)

Manhattan Memories. Poetry. (1989)

Elsewhere In A Parallel Universe. Poetry (1992)

The Many Faces Of Passion. Poetry (1996)

Brimmed Hat With Flowers, (Multi-Tasking.com). Poetry (2000)

Table Of Contents.

Credits

Resonance.....Matrix 25, 2000
Diving For Calamari.....Matrix 25, 2000
Eating The Fruit Of Love.....Matrix 26, 2001
Drowning In My Dreams.....Matrix 26, 2001
Pineapple Express.....Matrix 26, 2001
A Vulnerable State Indeed.....Poetic Licence,
Poetry Today, 2001
Anne Of The Infinite Heart.....Remembering
Friends, Poetry Today, 2001
A Storm - - Passing.....The Next Best Thing,
Poetry Today, 2001
Orca Fading.....Here And Now, Poetry Today, 2001
Briar's Crossing.....When The Leaves Fall, Poetry
Today, 2001
Yesterday.....Tides Of Time, Poetry Today, 2001
The Night Has Been A Carrier.....Searching
Visions, Poetry Today, 2001
The Perfect Wave.....Dream International
Quarterly, 2001
Tomorrow Is Long Coming.....Dream
International Quarterly, 2001
The Watered Bed.....Dream International
Quarterly, 2001
Blue Blood.....Hartnell Review, 2001
The Scent Of Her Mind.....Dan River, 2002
Yesterday.....Voices Of Today, Poetry Today, 2002
Daffy.....A Walk With Me, Poetry Today, 2002
Reflection.....Symbols Of Life, Poetry Today, 2002

World Of Wet

The World of Wet

Huge mountains soar beyond imagination.
Secret caves exist where marine creatures
dwell & keep vigil for delectables.
This world of which I speak is the World of Wet
home of our ancestors -- a world affecting
climate changes & our survival on Earth.

The Ocean -- great moderator of heat energy
from our sun -- provider of sustenance for
immeasurable populations yet vile/treacherous
& unforgiving to those who choose not to heed
or respect her realm. One might come eye to eye
with a giant squid -- long tentacles streaming
while inking the water with a protective shroud.

Some underwater critters of the sea swim in
schools unaware of their predators in deceiving
seaweed or swaying kelp stalks dancing
to the currents of the ocean.

I experience strong tugs -- tides insistently
beguile me to glimpse extraordinary events
encountered only by species of the *benthos*.

I gaze into depths longing for a magical
submersible -- protection from pressures as I
explore an environment hostile to humans.
I imagine gliding in Ocean deep -- a sea filled
with luminous night creatures -- starfish/sea
hares/bright-eyed puffer fish/gentle sea cows
& rays butterflying past me in motion slowed
grace. The profundity of sound is overwhelming
subtle snaps & sizzles from small crustaceans --

warbles/grunts/croaks/pops/songs & clicks from legions of fish & mammals. Crystal clear sounds like castanets travel miles to communicate in deep waters. Giant mammals of the sea sing mermaid fantasies to each other. But these sounds of Nature are often masked by the throb of giant blades -- the ping of depth finders -- the low rumble of engines & oil exploration with uncontrolled subsea thunder -- all whose sources emanate from machines.
I shudder from the effects of man & shed saline tears as I foresee the future of the World of Wet.

Diving For Calamari

I've heard whispered stories
of a man with facile hands
which deftly break the water.
He is a drummer of the sea
using rhythmic timing for the grab.
Fluids fascinate this learned man
who dives for squid in waves
slapping at his sides before
he swims serenely with his hand
wet with a squirming mollusk.
Its long tapering penlike tentacles
stream behind as they swim by
pumping water seeking sustenance
which brings to mind the mind
of this Professor. He speaks
of Calamari cooked Italian style
& I am left with hunger
for a taste of something new.
I'll have to learn just how to eat
this squid by watching how he cuts
the meat & puts it in his mouth --
how I must masticate this delicacy
which once was such a mystery to me.
There's much to learn about the deep
whose soundings he has studied.
I hear he's learning how to surface
long enough to breathe & dive again
for squirming squid whose juices
tantalize him cooked Italian style.
But Spaniards also know the culinary
secrets of preparing squid -- bring it to
a boil & roll it in a wrap of crumbs &
fry or bake until the scent announces
it is ready for the feast.   Bon appetit!

The Watered Bed

I just opened a book --
one about Oceans & as I
observed worlds foreign to me
I gasped because I felt
the tug of belonging where a
watered bed awaited me.

We must adapt to breathe
in fluids as when wombed.
How do we breathe air once
born & is it painful? Or could
we grow gills & swim
in the middle of a dream.

As I read & absorb the strangeness
of an inner world where Oceans
dominate I am compressed by pressure's
power at greater depths & surface waves
crash against the shoreline of my
brain as if trying to reclaim me.

The Perfect Wave
(The Surfer & the Observer:
Both Sides of the Equation)

The Surfer.

A local flock of sea gulls raised their vocal
chorus of squawks/squeals & scolds
protesting my intrusion to the beach parking
area where I left my Woody station wagon.
Some flew overhead. Others perched on spots
they could find & strutted/bobbing their heads --
necks continuously swiveling eyes wide &
searching for specks of food or insects crawling
on the ground. They were a skittery & cautious
flock while an earned friend lighted at my feet.
He was Hoppy -- my one-legged pal who eagerly
awaited his morning treats of bread & scraps
from my table -- the treats I brought each
morning which had bonded us together. I tossed
a few morsels to his unimpaired family & flock
mates saving a bit for later & surveyed the
chilled morning's bounty before me.

The Observer.

Another dreary chilly morn. Turning up the
heater I went through my morning ritual of
bathing/brushing my teeth & turned on my
coffeemaker for a morning's strong brew.
Bundled in sweatshirt & flannels I sat at the
table -- window facing a low sea wall past the
parking lot. Ahhhhh a strong aroma reached my
nostrils & I held the mug closely warming my
hands while sitting at table waiting for the

surfer & his friendly pal -- a one-legged sea gull
who followed him around the sand & surf
leaving his other feathered friends behind -- at
least for awhile.

The Surfer.

A soft glow in the East promised a pristine day.
Low marine cloud layer shrouded the coastline
as wisps of water vapors rose lazily just beyond
the breaking waves. Winter slowed the solar
heating engine & a closed cell rubber sheath
would insulate my body's warmth. Onshore
breezes blew lightly & three brown pelicans
rode the updrafts from breaking waves.
Singularly I greeted the beach that Winter's
morning as if keeping a bargain with Lady
Ocean. Respect me as I respect you & we shall
remain friends, -- forever.

The Observer.

The chilly morning invited me to cuddle but
there was no one to hold but my hot mug of
coffee. Sitting at the table facing the Ocean I
noticed the surfer had arrived & was changing
into his rubber suit. This was the part I loved
the best watching him undress while facing the
ocean & I fantasized at holding this stranger in
my arms taking the chill from my body. I
chuckled at the sight of his tight buns. Yet --
I could not understand the love of body surfing
that required such dedication in the frigid
waters of the Winter's dawn. Mission Beach,
San Diego, a haven for surfers & free spirits
called to the man obviously. He waded through

7

the shallow surf & rows of foam then dove too
high through the first big breaker. I watched
him get tumbled/churned/pushed as he sucked
for air. I saw his smile as his toes touched sand
& a sweet breeze soothed his lungs.

The Surfer.

The tide was in early flood stage & large swells
had come from the Southwest generated by
storms thousands of miles away. The Waves
were perfectly spaced in sets of four or five &
the break height was twice that of me. Through
the shallow spent surf I waded -- picking the
first big breaker & dove through much too high.
A monster wall of green water raced my way --
hissing/roaring towering/inescapable/sweeping
me into a cascading aquatic mayhem. I stood
choking -- faced the next advancing wave &
dove into it! Exhilarating! Sun now lofted
above the horizon warning me of day's duties
which yet awaited me. One last wave beckoned
to me -- maybe the perfect wave. I swam to the
breakline & turned towards shore. Another
monster lifted me as I accelerated to match the
wavefront speed. The ride was a gift for
perseverance. I smiled at my friend The Ocean
as I trudged up the beach to change unaware a
lady drinking coffee had been watching me all
the while. Overhead a flock of sea gulls sent
different messages near my wagon. Some
begging some scolding but ol' friend Hoppy
squealed with glee. He knew of parting scraps
& his gut was so soon empty again. He quickly
hopped about gulping gluttonously & once took
an offering from my palm as if to say I know we

are friends. Looking through the salt-speckled windshield I marveled at the magnificent expanse knowing this same Ocean reached the South China Sea. It teemed with life & energy & many things unknown. Perhaps one day the Ocean would share her secrets with me. I bid farewell until tomorrow as I slowly drove away my eyes cast seaward looking for the perfect wave.

The Observer:

I looked at him get out of his wet suit & slowly dress with a pair of soft jeans with turtleneck to match. He sauntered away -- Hoppy hopping behind him & I watched him occasionally reach into his pockets to give Hoppy another treat. I almost wished I was that sea gull reaching for a treat from this friendly & anonymous morning fantasy -- the surfer. Now -- in dreams I dive in the water hold tight to my swimmer when he rides the waves. I leave him for awhile to follow ships & see humans point at this aberration of another human at home in the ocean. My body is fluid & I blend with mammals who feel warm to my touch. We pass each other by & I feel no difference in emotions. I am invited to swim & race with them but even in dreams they exceed my efforts. I am new at this. New reverting to old memories & patterns of the sea. I have been captivated by the surfer's love of the ocean & I have fallen in a world of wet. I am becoming someone else & I feel the slap slap of the water all around me pushing me out further with the tide. Where is my friendly fantasy? I am too far out to swim back & now the dream becomes a nightmare of being pulled down into a cavernous vent where boiling water awaits me. Wait! I see him swimming towards me.

He wraps his arm around my chest bringing me closer to shore & Hoppy waits for him & me to walk on the sand beside him. Panting for air I wake up realizing I'd been in the sea & in dreams I had joined the surfer in his search for the perfect wave.

Appearances may deceive even the discerning.
No matter what your station blood runs red in
your veins. So where did this legend of Nobility
come from & the shade of Royal Blue? What do
Social Registers contribute to the tincture of
blood? Noblemen do not refract Sunlight & dire
circumstances can place one in a salt-water
coffin. It is the Ocean's currents which cloud its
waters with matter & metals changed to ions.
So depth alone cannot determine the turbidity
which affects Light's spectrum. Salt water
slowly decomposes all substances & what are we
who once crawled from the sea. Now we ride in
capsules & breathe cleansed Earth's
atmosphere. Confinement in submersibles can
try the best of men. Space is that precious
preventative of claustrophobia for some
humans. Air is a prerequisite for all mammals..
& what of depth's pressures crushing body
forms & hulls alike. Strained compressions
seek entrance with compelling force to reclaim
its airborne offspring. What of divers who
suffer cuts at water's depths bleeding blue from
wounds deceiving even the discerning.

Coursing Through Our Veins

There is a sparkling wilderness
reflecting our origins in briny
solutions coursing through our veins.
A saline solution of ionized particles
covers three fourths of Earth's surface
& streams through every human life
form. I see blood ooze from a tiny
cut in my finger & ponder the mystery
of evolutionary ladders.

Irony rules. Humans have conquered
the world while the Ocean remains
Earth's master -- its presence --
a shimmering palladium. I ride
& plunge the waters which can raise
ships with little effort -- crash them
with no thought into cavernous
troughs like playthings.

I am in wonderment of moving
Earth plates/volcanoes creating
islands/internal waves in the Ocean
boiling water at five miles deep.

All remain enigmas to our
irrepressible curiosities.
What is this aqueous entity
covering most of our planet & why
do its components run through
my veins -- my veins & yours?

Living Hot – Living Deep.

It's the seawater --
the way some objects float
while others sink
down
      down
            down
into the cold darkness
down
      down
            down
where pressure dominates
down
      down
            down
where saltwaters warm
become hotter in fissures
between cracks of crust
where scalding saline liquid
is spewed forth
from hydrothermal vents[1]
hidden in its depths
appearing as shimmering
upside-down waterfalls.
Roiling boiling water scorches
whatever cannot stand
these hostile habitats.

Great quantities of bacteria
in shooting geysers
cloud the water column
spreading dense colorful
carpets over crustal surfaces.
Fanciful culprits --

executing Nature's magic
using elemental ions creating
energy to synthesize[2]
organic material. These are
the primary producers
of mutuality performing
in ocean's nethermost reaches.
Envision odd life-forms
proliferating -- living
in a dark world devoid
of sunlight but awash
in mineral compounds.
Shrimp/crab/mussels
giant clams/pink jellyfish
& red worms are but a few
of these strange denizens
thriving in the abyss.

Symbiosis[3] -- a mutualism
enjoyed between slithering
scarlet worms trading internal
habitat to billowing bacteria
for digestive tract & nutrition.
Red tube worms brim with hemoglobin
growing six feet tall in luxurious
thickets. Waving in thermal currents
they appear as underwater rose gardens
ablaze with tinctures of crimson.

Thermophiles are bacteria which live
in blast furnace-like temperatures
on the ocean's bottom. That is living
hot & living *deep*. Their genes unlike
any other may not be bacteria at all --
but a new form of microbial life.

Archaea named *the ancient one* --
a one-cell microbe -- able to live
without sunlight or organic material.
If so -- where did they originate?
If so -- why not on other planets?

1. Hydrothermal vent: Deep sea vents or chimneys occur along
mid-ocean ridges and tectonic plate junctions where plumes of
mineral rich superheated water erupt from fissures in the sea
floor. Heated by molten material below, the temperature of the
water emanating from a vent can range from 77 to 762 degrees F.
The intense pressure at the vent depth some 2500 meters (8,100
feet) below the sea surface allows the water temperature to rise
above its boiling point and remain as a liquid, hence the term
superheated. Because vent hot water is less dense than
surrounding cold sea water, buoyancy continues to drive it
upward. Superheated water slowly escaping from a
hydrothermal vent appears as an upside-down waterfall.
2. Synthesize: The production of a substance by the union of
chemical elements. In this case, chemosynthesis: The process by
which organisms, without sunlight, use heat, water, and
inorganic chemicals, such as hydrogen sulfide to create organic
matter. In contrast, photosynthesis is the process by which
plants use the sun's energy, water, and carbon dioxide to create
organic material and oxygen.
3. Symbiosis: The intimate living together of two dissimilar
organisms in a mutually beneficial relationship. The red tube
worm contains a special protein that binds to the hydrogen
sulfide in the vent water and transports it to the bacteria living
within the worm's body. The bacteria then use the blood-bound
sulfide along with carbon dioxide in the water to create organic
carbon within the worm, thereby providing nourishment.
Ref: Prager, Ellen, J. With Sylvia A. Earle, 2000. "The Oceans",
McGraw-Hill, New York, New York.

Hydroplaning in the Salt Marsh

A gentle sea breeze riffles through shoreline saw grass[1] stands lining South Carolina's salt marshes. Rich ocean estuaries for small schooling fish lure many hungry predators. Along gently sloped coastal plain as the tide ebbs broad mud flats become exposed & an extraordinary event unfolds. Sea birds vie for front position as they have a vested interest in things to come.

A group of porpoises[2] gather at the mouth of small tidal stream for a coordinated attack. Their blow holes mist rainbow arcs against morning's sun. Echolocating fish schools in turbid channel they execute a tactical maneuver. Each porpoise one half-body length behind the other -- a ballet of bodies stagger to the right like combat airplanes flying formation & they race up the shallow salt creek. Skimming along mud-slick bottom with more than half their bodies out of water these marvels create additive bow wave ever larger to the right crashing upon mud flats ejecting fish to flop & flounder streamside. A sea eagle has watched the pursuit with interest timing his swoop perfectly to steal a fish & not get caught himself. Using excellent above water vision porpoises shimmy up mud banks & snatch up stranded silver fish. For reasons unknown these porpoises always run up the banks on their right sides. Over time their teeth on the right become worn down to nubs from chewing as much mud as fish.

Such is the consequence of Nature.

The porpoises take turns feeding & females
teach their calves techniques of high-speed
hydroplaning. A skill passed by generations.
As the tide turns to flood scavenging sea birds
flock to feast on floundered fish leftovers & pick
flats clean. With smiles permanently embodied
on faces well fed porpoises feel frisky & frolic
with friends & family as they play chase games
showing off acrobatic antics. These are the
Atlantic bottlenosed dolphin[3] among the most
inventive & intelligent hunters in the sea.
They use their intellect to survive & ever
changing strategies to suit their environment.
As they wobble up the mud banks it is as if they
are evolving into the land creatures they once
were. Some 50-million years ago their ancestors
of air-breathing mammals ventured into the
sea. To follow dolphins in the wild is to discover

The World of Wet.

1. Saw grass: any of various sedges (as of genus Caladium
effusum) of marsh grasses in southeastern coastal plains of the
U.S. having linear leaves and edges of leaves set with minute
teeth often sharp enough to cut human flesh.
2. Scientific Classification of Dolphin and Porpoises.
Class: *Mammalia;* animals that suckle their young.
Order: *Cetacea;* carnivorous, wholly aquatic mammals.
Family: Odontoceti; toothed whales, including dolphin and
porpoises. The smallest of the toothed whales.
Genus: Delphinidae; dolphins & porpoises.
Species: Tursiops truncatis; Atlantic bottlenose dolphin, ergo;
Flipper.
3. The Difference Between Dolphin & Porpoises. Dolphins are
generally described as having a "beak" and conical teeth, while
porpoises are blunt-headed and have spade-shaped spatular
teeth, but no "beak".

Orca[1] Fading

Sleek black backs dorsal fins
bright white bellies
fluke tails churning
dolphin-like swim as
blowholes billowing fine salt
spray. L-Pod[2] in the hunt --
count them now --
twenty-nine in autumn.
L-Pod -- a family of killer whales[1]
nearly permanent residents
of Puget Sound & The Straits
Of Georgia struggle
against the obstacles of man.
Over fished are the waters'
precious sustenance caused
by more than fifty years of gill nets
poachers & international sea-born
fish processing factory ships
raping fishing grounds
like clear cutting virgin forests.
I hear the wails of whales
as toxic chemical runoffs
from upstream river water
sheds come from farms
& cities alike. Chemical
fertilizers weed
& foliage killers dominate
& takes toll on immune
system as mammals' energy ebbs.
Many miles are traveled
each day by L-Pod Orcas
searching for salmon
& other schooling morsels.

Energy's return is negative.
L-1 Oscar/L-Pod bull
leads his family & joiners
to river mouths in search
of spawning-bound salmon.
The hunt is unrewarding
as the Pod turns south
for bay & inlets --
one last chance for the fall
run of Chum salmon.
The quest is disappointing
as the Pod ailing & weakened
heads seaward turning south
to winter in coastal California
waters. Spring again -- L-Pod
returns home for summer grazing.
Count them now --
twenty-three in number.
The Pod grieves their loss --
as I do. These amazing creatures --
right here on my island door step
belie their common name.
So here I am -- speaking out
for the Orca/the ecosystem
& against an international
bureaucratic constipated system.
Is anyone listening?

1. Scientific Classification of the Orca, Killer Whale. Class:
Mammalia. Order: Cetacea. Family: Odontoceti. Toothed
marine mammal who suckle their young.
2. Three Pods of Orcas, killer whales, reside in Puget Sound and
The Straits Of Georgia, J, K, and L-pods. Each whale in each Pod
in the order of their birth is assigned a sequential number for
tracking and scientific data gathering by an international
cooperative program managed by the Center For Whale
Research, Friday Harbor, San Juan Island, Washington.

Siren's Song

Lately
marker buoys appear as *Sirens*
depicting dangerous currents
dwelling beneath a point of view.

Learning to float
is a prerequisite to swimming.
Recognizing signals allow early
warnings of treacherous motions.

Ballast
an adjustment of necessity --
a perfect balance
the objective.

Watch out
for hidden rocks. Lie on your back
but stay your course. Don't let
the waves overwhelm you.

Tranquility
comes to those who close their ears
to Siren's song & search for depth
behind alluring sparkling facades.

The Intruders

The Weeds Of Death

Count them if you can --
those roots settling
in an earth of flesh.
Incursive growth
wild as weeds
spread slowly on
the body's trellised frame.
Chemo cocktails
contain this evil garden
from proliferation.
Stochastic conclusions
have helped penetrate
the realm of the invader.
One by one those roots
are separated by the scalpel
leaving behind raw cells
growing a healthy coat
in its wake. I am privvy
to the healing of a matter
whose mystery lies
in the way it multiplies.

Between Two Worlds
(Between Two Lovers)

1.

She: So many questions to ask when you come
back. So many memories to recall Time.
to test our training & technique in
visualizing auras of each other.

He: *My brain is active -- cramped with*
self-induced full color images & shapes
cubed/balled/oblonged & pyramidal
dimensions. All movement is experienced
slow & flowing & touch is real.

2.
(Operation Morning: Pre-anesthesia)

He: *I am being prepared for surgery &*
injested some Valium to calm my nerves.
My brain awaits removal of the intruder
yet I still visualize. Focus allows me to
view my surgeon & the empty chair
reserved for you my beloved. I see your
rising light from the right side of the
operating table & then I am under --
deeply under. Colors permeate my mental
palette. Pastels are dominated by lights
bright & sparkling silvers. Rounded
cornered auras slowly flow between
densities & translucencies. Graceful
& fluid is the dance of movement but
sensitivity to touch has been diminished.
Yet I feel a light kiss on my lips while an

oblong aura leans over the table & my
right hand is held most tenderly.

3.
(While Under Anesthesia)

He: *Deep into another world I feel your body*
lay on mine & our tight embrace is
followed by a kiss intense in its emotion.
Again I see your light & you are soft upon
my upper body where the veil separates
me & the outer world is removed. I am
out in space & view the planets. Spheres
of various sizes & pastel colors have
moons orbiting their Heavenly bodies.
Auras dance before me shifting shapes &
roundness. Some are dense and others
thinly outlined. Moon rings are slightly
darker than the planet & I feel escape
from Earth's electromagnetic &
gravitational fields.

She: Ah my love -- allow me to interrupt your
sharing of these visions for some I have
induced with meditation. Yesssssss my
love you feel my hand & body lay on
yours as you are slowly being led to a safe
place in your mind but little did we know
the trips you'd take with such limited
practice just between us. I'm not
surprised. Your mind is awesome in its
power & you stun me by the touch of your
lips on mine though we are half a country
far apart. But space cannot separate
a loving contact such as yours & mine.

24

4.
(The Episode: Seizure.)

He: *I see darting flashes of brights: vivid reds*
orange & misshapen auras. Some form
like cirrus clouds -- long streaked horse
tails stream by speeding winds with
jagged edges/sharp points & spiralling
vortices. All dart with rapid movements
while others travel in random tracks.
Now I feel the threat of zooming shadows
which hover over my body then disappear
in an unknown period of Time. Time oh
Time moves unknowingly to me & colors
gradually soften to soothing greens/
blues & the colors of Earth. Motion
almost coasts to a halt & I feel a
comforting breeze flow over my life's form.
Ahhhhhhh Reassurance! I begin to see
an aura known to me. It rises from the
chair on my right, where she told me to
place it. The shape shines with a familiar
lighted edge I've known before & I adore.
She touches my hand & I gently squeeze
hers back. She hovers over my right side
& slowly bends to softly kiss my cheek.
The episode has passed. I am reassured
& my anchor deeply set. I am secure. Soft
pastels return dominated by the bright
points of light -- sparkling silver shapes
with radiance glowing at their edges move
with fluid grace & flow. I've regained a
safe haven known well to my
subconscious. I rest.

5.
(The Light Sleep State)

He: *My lover's aura fades as do those pastel*
colors which gained & lost focus. My
mental energy is spent. Concentration
has deserted me yet I begin to sense
familiar sounds/voices & movement
about me. A trusted intonation --
manly in pitch speaks quietly to me. His
rich timbre asks questions which trigger
association. My love/family/friends
the boat. Crusing. Islands. The Ship to
Shore radio. A squeezed hand for yes.
Nothing for no. The trusted one says
softly that I will awake tomorrow & I
believe him. I feel your breasts hard
on my chest & the light brush of your
kiss lingering on my lips. We are
comfortable in our space & tomorrow we
will be just fine.

She: Sleep has caught you in its clutch. It's
been three days my love & I think of your
body which awaits you. I've seen the
globes which comforted you. I've seen the
beauty "out there" -- was tempted to stay
& join the globes which once had
welcomed me but I was pulled to Earth
against my will & my wish to explore
worlds other than my own. I pray this is
not the case with you that you've chosen
life instead -- Life as we know it now.
My aura no longer glows in your mind. I
trust my love lives in your heart. A hand
squeeze telegraphs responses. Spirit

takes a holiday & the hotel is Rest Of The
Mind which may entice you with release.
They say you move -- make yourself
comfortable & will awaken tomorrow.
Your skin shines a healthy glow but you
sleep on & I need you Mi Profesore.

6.
(The Awakening)

He: *I see light! I am aware of voices &*
movement! Some tones are known but not
placed. A warm glow enters my body. I
feel the tender touch of her hand & lips
meet mine. I hear a family member call to
me -- I must awaken! My cocoon is safe
& I ponder possibilities. I hear calls
again & strain to open my eyes but can't.
Ring, Ring, ah my cell phone pressed
against my ear. Hello my love?

She: Someone answers the phone & holds it
to your ears. I speak to you with loving
husky tones hoping to wake you from
three days of being *Elsewhere*. You are
awake & say hello. I say it's good to hear
your voice again. Your pitch is deep from
being silent but still you say you love me
& ask if anything is wrong. We laugh!
What else can we do when the one I love
has come back to this reality & me.
And now the story told in depth will
unfold slowly of your trek Between Two
Worlds. Between two lovers.

What?

The subtle invasion commences!
Possession privately propagates
Itself without warning --
secretly seeks silent passage
through microscopic crypts
& chasms -- conquering.
It follows like a shadow
ever closer -- invisible
to the naked eye -- perhaps forever.
I ponder what the composition of this
stealth invader is & why *It* has
chosen this vessel for engagement.

I am the one -- the intruder.
You don't know I exist
while I am suckling strength
from being. I am the encroacher --
the seed carried in the wind
of your embodiment
searching to permeate & take root.
I will take you in my time --
build strength to destroy barriers
you naturally possess -- ever growing.
I am the one without soul
ready to steal yours & everything
you are -- because I can. I am
presently the unknown quantity
hovering over the psyche sending
signals of imbalance. In time
you'll know my name. The war
has just begun. Prepare for battle.

When?

I have no sensibility when *It* entered my body --
found a niche actuated -- tangling tenacious
roots in my stomach wall. Learning the *When*
of the diagnosis & prognosis -- attacked my
attitude of invincibility. Denial impacted my
psyche & turned thinking upside down. There
must be an error in analyses or files. This must
be someone else -- not me! I am filled with
fierce anger -- sweet antidote for surrender --
the heat of volcanic fury erupts within me for
the battle to suvive & oust this alien presence
from my *being.*

Research & biopsies dictated *It* inoperable.
Treatments began immediately -- radiation &
chemotherapy each day & examinations
every Friday only to find *It* growing larger --
thriving on my tissue. My partner & I --
practitioners of Meditation & Visualization
seized the gravity of the prognosis & instantly
devised a strategy to attack this *Invader.* Our
mental & spiritual energies empowered by the
Universe -- focused like laser beams would
attack *It* using visualistic methods of root
pulling. We met each night -- fifteen minutes
on each occasion. *It* continued to grow from a
small circular pattern into a large egg-shaped
mass until the seventh set of scans & images
displayed an opening in the middle. I smile
because my partner had been pulling roots
there every night for weeks with a lighted
miners' hat to find her way amongst the field
of rooted stalks. *They* crawled on her fishing

boots -- wriggled frantically in gloved hands
as she manually wrapped *usurpers* with strings
of roots -- depositing *Them* in dead white blood
cells & excreted by the system.

The ninth set of scans & images showed a larger
hole in the center & the oval shape was about to
split into two parts -- left side larger than the
right. My partner encouraged increased efforts
to ensure separation of the whole & predicted a
dent would occur in the upper right hand side
as a result of our meditations.

The tenth set of scans & images verified our
success in visualization as *It* was now two parts.
We had broken through! Enthusiasm spurred
her on. She created with her imagination
a miniature machine & ploughed through rows
of stalks in my stomach. Tied in stacks *they*
were ejected -- wrapped in dead white blood
cells to be expunged by me at my leisure.

A hospital stay -- intense radiation &
chemotherapy -- integrated visualized root
pulling -- demonstrated the tide had turned
in my favor. The thirteenth set of scans &
images showed *It* diminished by half.
There was also a large dent in the upper right
hand side verifying my partner's early
prediction. A short respite was granted from
intense treatments as visualization remedies
continued & I prepare for the next assault on *It*.
There is no doubt there is a future in this
wondrous shared world of science &
metaphysics The end is near for *It*
        & I know *When*.

Where?

It's like a dark/damp/inviting cave
for an opportunistic spelunker invader.
A home to sink roots & grow
exponentially without restraint.
I've often thought of this variant
organism looking to usurp host provinces --
a parasitic alien whose appetites
cannot be appeased -- following
a grand design to overcome/mutate
& replace our species.

It has moved into my stomach walls
behind the pancreas. That's *Where*
refuge & lodging was gained
without my permission.
Ignored defenses of white soldier cells
attempting my rescue --
but to no avail. This strong
encroacher multiplies --
devouring my body as sustenance.
But I am a match for this transgressor.
A fighter! A believer in Faith!
A Visualizer! Pulling up roots
with my partner every evening.

Imaging & scans have caught
the pictures of rapid growth
& now a slow divided demise.
I can attest to belief systems
of the brain triggering help from an
Interconnected Universe. Radiation
& chemotherapy are allies --

part of my battle equation confronting
seemingly uninterested parties.

The originations of this assassin
remain mysterious entities
within my body & have altered
my attitude. I have gained prowess
using other parts of my mind
as my partner has nurtured
the metaphysical spirituality
of intangible Faith.

We will continue to attack *It*
until eternal remissivity prevails.
It will have to evolute
to a more convivial state
to be accepted by any human.

Who?

Who entered his body
& multiplied without conscience?
It is a warrior to be feared
this creeping crawler/this monstrosity
feeding on this man's body to propagate itself.
I have felt the pain/discomfort & fear
of a brave man & I proclaim that I will kill
this thing with my mind. I am trying --
believe me. Headaches come more often.
Stress strains patience & empathetical emotions
deplete my energy. In dreams -- I'm a killer --
murdering intrusive cells mercilessly
& then I am rewarded with occasional
remissions to my partner in the endeavor by
connected visualizations. We will *see*.

I am the Who you speak of so disdainfully.
Beware of the likes of me for you too may be
visited. Your flesh & bones are so inviting.
I could feed on them & grow in all directions. I
know it's You & Him plucking my roots while
visualizing. I grow weak from loss of embedded
tentacles. Of course the dreaded radiation &
vile chemos have done their part to slow & try to
kill me but there's nothing I fear more than
Faith which has engulfed me. I am
overwhelmed by omnipotent forces. I'm slowly
being dispossessed -- decimated without roots to
call my own.   I am disheartened as I am a
fighter too but alas -- not much longer.

How?

*It -- many call me -- a microscopic malformed
neoplasm cell metastasized from carcinoma
tumor in host's organ. Making my exploratory
voyage through neighboring tissues into
spacious stomach cavity embedding my roots in
connective tissues in abdominal walls. I see
the nearby pancreas & yearn for delightful
delicacy. But -- my feeding roots are secure as I
multiply millions -- for building cancerous
tumor -- if I can.*

*My parent tumor & others have been surgically
removed -- now wicked waves of radiation &
bitter brutal blasts of chemicals kill relative's
roots. I sneak/snuggle/seeking survival in
recess of cavity wall. I'm growing wide -- not up
like my parent & wonder why? Ah! A mutation
rapidly replicating Self. Maybe my mutation is
unique & as seeking continues I'm unfound --
Holiday! My host's radiation & chemotherapy
treatments have stopped & as the host grows
stronger -- so do I. Still thinking of nearby
pancreas & pleasant partaking.*

*Each week strange things happen.
Poking/prodding/probing/palpitating
& picture taking. Unpleasant encounters as I
query their hunt. Are they seeking me or others?
If I'm found can they render harm? Suddenly
hollow shiny steel sharpness pierces my core as I
struggle against strong suction -- unsuccessfully.
An empty space -- a red runny reminder of*

painful extraction. I sense something from
heritage. Oh! A biopsy bringing grievous
aching. My identity is in danger. Tests show
divergent differences displaying my kind like no
other posing prognosis problems. Amazing! I'm
inoperable! Two days following I began to feel
hot waves weaving through me & neighboring
cells as seemingly incessant inferno increased.
The heated waves suddenly stopped as started.
While alarmed -- assessing agony of roasted cells
my ingesting tentacles filled with unpalatable
blood leaving me undernourished & ailing.
Each day suffering same double-pronged attack
& at night two miniature beings assailed me by
root pulling. Armed with lights/boots & buckets
bundling wiggling roots tied fast with expired
white blood cells. Buckets full were flushed fast
& expeditiously expunged through host's waste
system. I soon suffer sever core casualties as
fatal foundations disappear & I'm left with an
ever expanding medial dilating hole. Day &
night assaults persist. I split into two parts --
the left larger than the right as weakening
magnifies. My night miniature mystical
marauders of host species -- a gender each. A
ruthless female attacks wearing miner's head
lamp/hip-boots & with bewitched root-pulling
machine consuming continuous rows remaining
in my right half. Weekly images show my slow
demise delighting miniature hosts/loved ones &
friends alike. I'm ailing & failing -- weakening
& tiring as is my host. Who will prevail?
A short respite from waves & chemicals but not
from nightly pestilent pulling impositions. The
host is strengthened & I remain weakened by

*nightly root pulling. Sudden sizzling cells
cooked crisper by ever stronger waves of
radiation followed by foul feeding chemicals
further cripple my essentiality. Chemicals
& radiation's increased intensity are sharply
focused sieges. Six days running -- rest one
& six more days running. Gasping -- grasping
no more. Enter the Pale Horse* -- It entered
nothingness!* Host/loved ones & joiners
jubilantly rejoice!

*The Pale Horse: One of the Four Horsemen of the Apocalypse.
Death. " I looked & behold a pale horse; and his name that sat on
him was Death".

Why?

Disease darken doors of many -- impairing
human organisms -- diminishing body's
defenses & denaturing internal regulators.
Speculations & some truths suggest I brought
this blight upon myself. Increased stressors &
state of mind -- exposure to toxic chemicals --
ionizing radiation viruses & hereditary factors
accumulated rendering my body vulnerable to
lurking seeds of *It*. Extrinsic growth springs
silently -- siphoning sustenance while normal
cell propagation is lost. Abnormal cells cluster
into a large mass conquering healthy tissue.
New sprouts of deviant intruder continuously
proliferates as *It* seeks & destroys normalcy.
Tiny masses of aberrant protoplasm interacting
among factors become multi-factorial
sequentially mutated processes producing
neoplasm malignancy. In multiplicities *It*
flourishes -- killing me -- if *It* can. Why does *It*
exist? Why was message imprinted on mind &
matter to choose me as *Its* quarry? Why do
some suffer the siege of *It* while others seldom
undergo any afflictions at all? Why must we be
constantly challenged to survive in a world
beset with knowledge? Apparently *It* grows
knowledgeable as well. *It* too is a survivor
evolving & adapting to changing environments
battling to multiply & populate *Its* Universe of
Mind & Matter -- Matter with direction &
thought. Somehow all things come & go for
underlying reasons. Some are understood while
others not -- trying my credulity.

The long war waged nearly a year. Many
battles fought -- winning most -- losing some &
experiencing energy exhaustion.

Then suddenly Saturday Springtime Surprise --
It was not to be found. Images were absent of
cancerous growth. Rewarded remission present
as I sigh with relief & smile as loved ones
friends & joiners clamor closer -- celebrating &
rejoicing our victory. But did we win the war
or another battle? Are there others hibernating
awaiting another Spring? Another question --
so many unanswered. Brain's ability to fully
comprehend unfathomable mysteries persist.
Are all things possible in the dark matter of
the mind -- dark matter invoked to explain the
unexplainable -- while pondered puzzles piece
together bits of knowledge becoming wiser as
constant flux remains. Why does this change in
our transitory world befuddle me? I accept all
things exist for a purpose & are somehow
interrelated -- another unexplainable. So -- is
Why the question or the answer?

Probes

The mind can cut corners
sift through facades
laden with hyperbole.

It is a tool -- sharp if used
discriminately to decipher
codes of linguistics.

There are probes of the body --
intruders of unwilling flesh
prodded by physicians.

Cutting demands analysis
based on observation.
& critical expertise.

Be wary of the knife
if it is a threat but welcome
the knife if it is to heal.

The sword of words
can slice through love
leaving soul cold & desolate.

Intense is the probe of *Phallus*
when welcomed with the wall
of facades finally down & dewed.

So speak softly & interpret
words spoken in earnest
& fidelity will be a given.

Helpful Healing Hints

I am amazed that we function
at all much less demonstrate
intricate reasoning powers
& conclusive thought.

The knowledge base of the
complex human body is
microscopic when compared to
sophisticated man-made systems.

Medicos & alchemists are our
body & mind menders but the heart
of love/positive thought & *Faith*
can manifest miracles.

Garnering strength from loved ones
& friends -- the door is slammed
on the foot of a demon of despair
trying to enter consciousness.

Trigger the brain with pulsed
Positivism. Ask for help from
The Universal Gods & feel *Faith's*
vibratory essence enter you to heal.

Becoming.

When Eyes See Without Seeing

I have been slaughtered
quartered/dominated
disrespected & displeasured
but I have escaped the grip
of thieves seeking to steal
my mind. I feel the line
get loose -- that line connecting
to the source of *Light* & I am
left for blind -- stickless
& shiftless in a world of dark.
The *Light* is dimming slowly.
I sense it behind the lid
of observation. Dusk thickens
& my insight quietly
& slowly gives birth
to another mode of seeing.
I open my lids & see the *Light*.

The Process

I am being fused to another
by a force which demands Oneness --
that supposed theory which attracts
its counterpart explainable by logic
& observation. That energy
which seeks to exchange its mask
for one of matter constantly confronts
the face of its Creator. Those tiny
particles but not particles at all
but waves -- speed the face
of tenses while producing
altered states & functionality.
Ah but we are human & fallible
in this mysterious sea of aggregates
contained within a dot of consciousness.
I yearn for clarity but only Faith
can pan the Light on this obscurity.
Humbled -- I become one with the *flow*
swaying & swimming inside of me
fighting the waves which will win
& finally change me into something else.
I pray -- that the arms of my Creator
will embrace my counterpart & make us
recognizable to each other though
masked we may be in this new play
of changing roles in the
incomprehensible act of *Becoming*.

Medathinking

The dot on the wall transfixes thought
temporarily -- an unwavering focus
slackening incessant sensory impulses
to the brain. The state of being
recognizes repose is required for renewal
as tension flows from mind & body
seeking relaxation -- an emptiness.
The inner eye sees what cannot be seen
when distraction distorts a compilation
of comprehensive images.

Senses serve as messengers to a body
which listens carefully.
Now our limbs tingle as one as we near
empyrean. The forehead becomes
an empty screen as brain waves
travel by visualizing being there --
a place imagined where
the quintessence of tranquillity
resides & peace reigns in the hearts
of those who will believe & love completely.

Flashing through uncharted mind-space
reaching the other side of *Elsewhere*
composure & Faith quiets
the *Intrabeing's* restless rebellions.
As weakened negativism slowly
withdraws -- the core of *Self*
is found across the realm of reality.
We float in a space without barriers
& the cycle is completed as we return
to our bodies -- *becalmed.*

Following Orders

Following orders without question
can be dangerous -- especially when
threats pierce you like a slick bullet
which opens you up to revelations
heard but not experienced before.
Confronting discovery can
traumatize the unsuspecting who
follows orders without question.
You can be penetrated by a swift
bullet faster than time or so it seems.
Experience teaches one not to follow
orders blindly -- to avoid that
intrusive bullet full of venom
but that is for the next time if one
should enter you spreading a poison
where none existed before. I now
question orders -- look for survival
within my own reason know bullets
are waiting to sever my bindings
& let the soul free from its crystalline
striations engraved & conceived by
a preordained destiny.

Needle.
    Thread.
        Eye.
            Fabric --
yet persistence pushes
Time's fiber through lids
which blink survival.
Time.
    Days.
        Hours.
            Linger --
like a stalled
storm warning.
Over the horizon
the weft of a blue
ribbon sky brings
reassurance.
Morning.
    Energy.
        Fresh.
            Promise --
light bursting
through sheers --
Sun denuding
night shadows
& threatening
trepidation
of seeing
what has been sown.
Hoe.
    Seed.
        Back.
            Soil --

Earth's orbit of sun
dictates seasons
for agrarian optimism
while Mother Nature
determines fate.
Wet.
    Dry.
        Weed.
            Pestilence --
each day -- light 'til dark
laboring like red ants
undaunted by
uncontrollable obstacles --
sweat covered
bowed bodies trudge.
Harvest.
    Sun.
        Combine.
            Prayer --
as storm clouds gather
& grain pours
like a golden river
to a sea of eighteen
wheeled monsters
creeping towards destiny.
Patching.
    Hemming.
        Binding.
            Mending --
rebellion's birth & causes --
seeking a union
of commonality
with cycles --
sowing compatibility
into the weft
of life's materiality.

Looking.
      Searching.
            Hoping.
                  Despairing --
seeking solace
in abundance
without guilts
knocking at the door
of conscience.
Blindly.
      Sorrowfully.
            Respectfully.
                  Humbly --
pondering the reasons
for imbalances --
seeing the eye
of the needle shrink
for those without vision.

Optical lenses help
to a degree startling users
seeing faults within
which move like
tectonic plates
eternally grinding.
The reality of truth
is difficult to tolerate
without sensitivity
& boldness to balance
the burden. At times
the reaping of seeds
can be a lesson in --
Imagination.
      Perception.
            Comprehension.
                  Determination!

The Seed Of Hope

Summer is here at last!
Flowers bare their faces
shamelessly. Diversity
flourishes everywhere.
Colors vibrate to the sun --
quiver with life & sensuality.
Crazed by scents & juices
insects fly, crawl, buzz,
around these rouged harlots.

The Dance of Life
continues. So it is when
Winter's thoughts intrude
you see the death of plants
& blossoms on the vine
& leaves fall crackling under
shoes & boots. But know ye
all who think of death
that it is but a cycle

of another change & Spring
will come to prove me right.
The plants will push their
stems through earth & bud
before your eyes just as
the years will grant you life.
It really is perspective
don't you know. It is the soul
which sees beyond the veil.

The Scent Of Her Mind

Impossibilities seemingly exist
within the realm & reality of *now*.
Explanations appear rational
in unillumined subterranes
where hungry snakes undulate
under careless cemented surfaces.
Decay rises like a baleful ghost
waving toxic & virulent fumes.
She walks warily -- mindful of cracks
& potholes exuding corrosion's stench.

She has smelled this effluvium
in different environments --
felt the fangs of reptilian ruptures
open cavities where mind buried
the bones of past uninvited crawlers
of consciousness. She has fled
the gore of game with nothing to show
for her pain but the welts of wisdom.
Tonight she types as if possessed
& her armpits wreak with sweat

of Karmic servitude. Her brain balances
the meld of a *Force* without & she tilts
her head to listen to songs of alien resonance.
She vibrates to this tuning fork fondling
her senses & nerves & she responds.
She smells a scent so sweet -- so palpable
the perfume dances to her skull
& she is drunk with the power & knowledge
that she has become a flower opening --
yes opening to *Light & Resurrection*.

My Favorite Shade Of Thought

Swept away
by a fickle breeze
to ease
its fall
the leaf
nods & dips
its tinted
Autumn shades
of wrinkled dry
a wry reminder
of its season
coming to a close
until next Spring
a leaf
distinctive
in its curve
its veins
its tilt
will nod with wind
at my discernment.

Memory Is A Matter Of Matter.

We die a little everyday in many ways.
Amazing is the concept that life
depends on dying just a little here
& there within the human body.

There is an area on flesh which itches
constantly. You scratch & rub seeking
release -- nerves not having yet
sent signals to the brain. Finally
you feel unbound & then the pain.

Now fresh flesh is abraded. A scab
has formed protecting tissue.
Underneath the scab you gently peel
away a new formed layer is exposed
alerting senses you are witness
to the birth of an epidermis.

As skin grows it knows where it belongs.
The path predestined by a memory
& process working on a lower level --
a level not seen but felt.

Another crust develops protecting
pink tissue once again while brain
& body have strengthened their
immunity to all infectious intrusions.
Amazing is the notion that one must die
a little everyday to live.

Containers

In spaces between particles
& waves dwells an emptiness
occupied by waiting souls.
Thought bounces off others
lingering & my mind is
enriched by sudden inspiration.
But I must dodge destructive
debris shooting through
Universe's constant birthing
& dying over & over again.
Invisible souls seek union to
become something new. All this
within an essence searching
for stability amidst the chaos
of creation.

Contained in a place of warmth
I am nourished. Growing --
becoming a fetus cradled in a
placenta of wet rocking to & fro
as song sounds lull me to sleep
slowly. Soon it will be time & I'll
be born -- again. My host hurts.
It's the growth straining back
& womb. Her stomach stretches
as I kick for space *to be.*

Married young. Bore two children.
My flesh. My heart. My legacy.
They matured -- married --
moved on. Put me in a retirement
home -- neglected. Escaped to
the streets -- widowed & penniless

losing contact with family. Memory
is almost gone & occasional
remembrances have become
unbearably painful. It's been years
& I am now an old woman. Streets
have become my home. Weather is
both my friend & enemy. Getting
weary -- even a cane cannot disguise
my limping gait. Shelters are
crowded & danger lurks in every
corner. Food is scarce yet I live on.
Why? I'm ready to go -- now!
This is coming to an end. I have
traveled life enough. I must pass
on -- leaving material behind
in an aging container.

A street weary woman with a dumpster
for her home has been identified
by missing persons as one who passed on
in the cold. But now she is reunited with
the children. Her remains lie in state
in another container while family mourns.

Rest in peace Mother -- they cry & I hear
the echo resounding in a space of particles
& waves occupied by other waiting souls.

Flight From Fury

Meditating on past
accumulated tormentors
& suppressed resentment
hatred grew into a third eye
looking inward & outward
blinding me with furies stronger
than any storm wreaked
by Nature. Shuddering under
violent forces repugnance
grew into a form larger than
my body bursting through
skin escaping into the world.

With guilt I now travel
where the wind blows
gathering remnants of
my hatred before contagion
gets out of hand.
Collecting garbage unwittingly
spewed upon the innocents
is my quest in life now.
Wisdom has me wading
through resistance borne
of habit. I feel a metamorphosis
transforming me. My feet fly
forward & I follow the path
laid before me feeling light
full of love -- accepting
responsibility at last.

Behold! A beautiful butterfly
has emerged from its chrysalis.

How To Become A Lady

It's her defiant walk
& eyes which talk
those lines she writes
that sometimes bite
with feminist
dedication.

This is a woman
who has not learned
the style that she
has spurned
most of her life.
A woman controlled
for years whose tears
let loose the noose
around her personality.

But she has gone too far
to be that free identity.
So back to school
she goes. She knows
it's time to take a chance --
change her stance.

Romance has room to bloom
one day for the lady
as she quietly enters
the lounge with grace
& social bearing.
She joins her friends
averts eyes to all others
demure -- for sure
while within a wildfire rages.

Once Again With Fervor

Ye s-s-s-s-s-s-s-s
do me again like you did
on the train to *Elsewhere.*
Ki-s-s-s-s-s-s-s-s
me with lips soft as silk
with searching
tip of your tongue.

I've been severed from
myself since I have
met you. The shadow
dressed in black is apropos
for me *in absentia* & only
you can spark the eyes
with life which have
dimmed to an allusion
of what was.

Do me again with fervor
like you did on the train
to *Elsewhere.* Kiss me
with lips soft as silk
searching the tip of my
tongue. I've been absent
from myself since I have
met you. I've become
a woman once dressed
in black now waiting
for the breath of life
gowned in white.

Things To Do

Now let me see.
That box by a club chair
should be removed
to improve my neatness
but then those two skirts
will be left undone
if not seen so I can make
a drawstring seam
without haste to
hold a tie inside the waist
& buttonholed fold.

Now look at the chair.
That red wool sweater
lying there with the holes
made by moths now covered
with contrasting cloth
cut into heart-shaped patches.
I've made a batch of these
to please the eyes from scraps --
fabrics now doing double duty.
A green sweater lies next to it
on the chair with its three hearts
covering other holes & next
to that is my brown velvet top
which needs mending on two hems --
a reminder by its visual presence.
Ah & there's the misplaced jeans
I have been looking for
under the paper stacks & under
jeans my old black slacks
pinned with four cut out hearts
to cover holes made by

the same moths I suppose.
Now near my chair
my old recliner --
are piles of file folders waiting
to be checked -- oh my stiff neck.
Will tell you more another day.
I have a fleck in my left eye
which interferes with sight.
My hope tonight
was I might get more accomplished.
But such is the foresight of
a slight procrastinator. I've been
through much this troubling year.
It's the *Becoming* that's a brutal
touch to a person such as I.

What do you think?
One must admit after reading
my long list that I am short
of being organized. Surprised?

The Screening Room
(Thinking About Thought.)

I have
no Time values
nor measurements
to clock galvanics
lighting
up my mind.

Crouching
behind gray
I *become*
startling me
into thought
& movement.

The *I* jumps
distances of
miraculous
proportions &
divines concepts
foreign -- hidden

underleaf
of observation.

Once Upon A Dream.

What Is Life Without A Dream?

A nightmare.
Amaranthine night.
Bone chill.
The loneliness
of space -- solitary.
Unutterable pain.
A never healing cancer.
Bitterness biting brain.
Escaping to Xanadu.
But that does not quell desire.
An importunate dream burns.
Exacting fulfillment.
There is a polestar.
Pulsating probabilities.
An erratic throb.
Blood running its circulatory course.
The only recourse is Faith --
thinking in a Positive manner
even for those
who love beyond reason.

The Unknowing

Language can be a barrier
to lovers interpreting speak.
Voice & body
tell different stories.
It is his smile or frown
which warns
the weary woman
to unlock his brilliant psyche.
An impatient sigh
escapes her lips
quivering defensively
at her unknowing wrong.
Frustration fatigues
his mind & the forced
smile of her lover
is forgiven for he is
in the grip of his
personal physical hell
& his unknowing triggers
misunderstandings.
Determination
dogs them both & this alone
blooms the love
which struggles to survive
against most odds.
She sees *Faith*
dig its roots deep
within their hearts
& souls. *Certainty's*
canopy closes in
protecting them from
weather's weathered words.

Communication

Communication triggers my mind --
to comprehend & decipher the cipher.
The mind is like a Universe
not completely understood
& the mystery fascinates me.
Information/thought/feeling --
all tender fruits ripe -- waiting
to be picked for realization.
Time's hands move indifferently
when it is consumed by miscommunication.
Frustration mounts until a bell
of comprehension is rung inside my head.
Then coherent thought converges in mind
& I am showered with intelligible
articulation. Language intrigues me --
especially those words with many
meanings. It is the whispers
of seduction to the uninitiated --
the purring of innuendoes spilling
suggestions from swollen lips
intimating something sensual
or sinister -- according to the
listener's sophisticated insight.
Deciphering subtleties is like
perceiving the intentions
of the speaker -- & then
the listener may interject
their own interpretation
according to intellect & experience.
As for me & others of my predilection
I love a secret message in a sentence
spoken softly in my ear & then I smile. :o)

Waiting

You are the one
I cling to for our future --
for surely we were
matched in another
lifetime -- an Elsewhere
created by imaginists.
Our promises
were made before we met
in minds mindful
of thoughts which travel
incessantly through
a universe constantly
changing. You speak
& my heart quivers
pounds & stops
without warning.
Anticipation
of waiting for someone
or something
is like expectations
from seedlings
to blossom & bloom
into brightly painted
springtime faces.
We share & resonate
commonalties
each day twice
or more to manifest
the will
of a predestined
dawning of a dream.
Now we wait --
wait. Oh -- the waiting.

A Passion For Identity

Preserving identity
can be a tumult
of the soul. It is
the constant quest
for fairness among
genders/cultures
& egos. In the thicket
of hair on the brain
listen to the thumps
of clubs amongst
our ancestors
& notice nothing
has changed.

Weak men can dominate
strong women.
Their fists speak of
parental violence
crippling empathetical
emotions & ability
to communicate
they are the masters.
Ah! Such irony exists.
Loneliness lends itself
to abuse. Developed
dependence on a lover
or husband can quell
the spirit & kill the soul.
Whatever devices are
concocted in the minds
of such men -- clubs/fists
& knives are weapons
of governing males.

They lose in the end
the love of a woman &
a relationship of respect.

A man's subtle deception
of domination can be
a mental turning of the screw
tightening temples by
the purposeful warping of
the mind. Watch out for these
stealthy stealers of the *ego* --
they hide in dendrites waiting
to stamp their mark upon
your brain until submission
is an almost welcomed ploy
to be accepted.. One
remembers past encounters
with diabolical duelists
of the *psyche* & becomes
steel devoid of pain numbed
as if drugged by morphine.
A faithless entity to the nth
degree now wonders
whether sunrise will arrive
as scheduled or not at all.
For what is there to lose but
that satiny smooth thief
seeking to squish thought &
prevent you from savoring
the pleasure of your own identity.
Rare is the person who can
accept a partner without
custom tailoring to fit.
Men who are secure in themselves
reach out for love & tenderness
exuding warmth like the rising sun.

Anne of the Infinite Heart

She was already seated at my left
when I arrived that evening
for the workshop. Her smile
radiated from her heart & there was
an openness about her which
crumpled my defenses. She was
a vulnerable lady -- one who
empathized with others --
an additional burden for the wounded
mind. I have wrapped my arms
around her & she me -- exchanging
fortitude & understanding. She is
the Light which softens
my hardened heart but now miles
separate these sisters of the soul.
She's but a phone call away &
I feel her power when chaos threatens
to overcome me. We put on our stiff
upper lips -- talk about trivialities
while loneliness cries quietly
in the space within. Our voices
resound with responsiveness
enveloping us both with a recess
from habitual regressive thinking.
We never know when our tears
will turn into laughter but it does.
It is the joviality of release.
Three cheers for Anne's rare
qualities. She is the Sun which sets
each night on the east side of Heaven
leaving behind her mark of ebullience
& a smile lingering long after
the phone has been returned to its cradle.

Reflection

The hot midday sun burns
my back like embers as bright
sheen of sweat oozes & drips
from my body. Visuals dance
before my eyes through radiated
heat waves as I seek refuge
from Devil's furnace.
Thought processes run dim --
a brain brownout. Mind's eye is
clouded. I race to serene comfort --
my psyche in denial overload.

Big rock on shaded shores
beckons me -- my sanctuary.
River rapids run white &
drown me in their cacophony.
A salmon rests in an eddy
before moving upstream
to spawning grounds
to multiply & perish.

Dappled sun on river's surface
paints vivid memories.
A laughing young woman
full of life -- a handsome
family gleefully at play --
a graying couple
holding hands communicating
through years of tender touch.
Clouds pass overhead
blocking images like a curtain
separating acts in a stage play.

Sun reappears
& shadows spring to life
but players are but one.
The graying man
walks alone head down --
shoulders bowed in despair.
The river of life ran short
for his mate --
like the salmon
her cycle completed.
He joins me on shaded rock.
We have a striking
resemblance. Stories
of our losses are shared
as shadows grow long
like our faces.
His dark piercing
eyes search mine
with haunting looks
of deep questions.
Matching strides we stroll
along river's bank.
We stop at a quiet pool
& look into reflecting water.
I see only me.

The Temptation Of The Gods

Karma demands complete subjugation. I must *Be* what has been alluded to by vicissitudes visited upon me *constantly* in this life I know as Now. So I have submitted my will to you -- (oh gods who are judgmental in my parlor of ideology) for all of you to examine the scars & welts on skin worn like medals of honor/pain like a sickness of altered mind to fit some religious fervor taught to me when I was young & impressionable. Those stimuli are tattooed on brain -- those technicolored pictures from a long ago exhibition exist & live in the museum of my life.

Oh gods, you tempt me to live -- sending me an Adonis who desires & conjures Universes for me to explore with my crippled senses. He flaunts his beauty/his brains before me. You gods almost make me believe that sin is really ready for reality but those imprintations are dug deeply in my skull/brain & mind so I enact my actions in faultless dreams where dark/damp dreary images exist in an underworld which I occupy in a space as small as an imagined particle or as large as the Universe itself. It is here I can indulge -- survive my other self intact & scoff at gods. I thumb my nose at society & sit by the side of my beloved -- savor his presence as he does mine -- howl at each nightly phase -- that damn moon which calls me to the hunt. See how I wave my tail good-bye to inhibitions & the gods -- my Karma which shackles my life into a box called an IM in my computer.

The Head Mistress

Vicious tongues abound
gossiping with lip sync
& latitudinarian
linguistics. Some are
grasped from the halls
of learning. Those
muscular movements
emit from mouths
clenched in irony.
Oh to be a tongue
a sooth-saying tooth
protracting instrument
of wisdom but tongues
are capricious
salivating at the taste
of good wine & sauces
served with a chef's
sense of a balanced
coup de'meal.
If one is famished
though any place
will do to chew & it
will be a feast of fare.
So if you see me sit
in the sidelines of
written oratory
watch me digest
exotic recipes eaten
in public domains
though privacy
is preferred any time
of day or evening when
dinner is being served.

The Barracuda Box

Beware of boxes
with teeth of bone.
One never knows
where to insert
one's curiosity.
Beware of fish
whose redolence
may tantalize.
Seduction is
a prelude to
surrender & a
conquest. Both
pay the price of loss
or gain if each
is left a taste of
what one was
before the plunge
into the magic
of the moment.
The nose twitches
at the perfume
of a memory.
You've been
tattooed by
the teeth
of your beloved.

Eating The Fruit of Love

Come! Take my hand!
Look beyond the clouds.
Uncover the sky & me.
We have bitten the apple
& it was sweet -- juicy.
Now the forests & limbs
of vined circumstance
present obstacles & we
swing to escape from
canopies which block out
the Light. The Garden
is growing wild but bees
have flown elsewhere
seeking honey stolen in
the night. I am a Lady
who roams the Garden
& snakes of aggression
seek to distract me but
my course has been
plotted & mapped for me.
I wait for the full moon
to appear & wait for
howls which always
pierce the air with
urgency. Each night
I wait for *him* for it is
then I come alive when
he puts his lips on my
flesh & drinks of the fruit
of the holy Garden. Yes.
For holy is the fruit of love
which quenches the thirst
of the living dead.

A Storm Passing

It is cool & silent.
Rambling tree branches
slow dance while wind
quietly winds around
my waiting thighs
& still is cool & silent.
The touch of my lover
lights up the sky. His
hand radiates power
& my body sings.
The groan of my throes
rumble like the sounds
of thunder. Our
passion shrieks to be
heard -- a crescendo
peaking beyond the
bounds of mortals.
Our hearts -- touched
by the gods -- melt
like warm chocolate.

Hush now.

Do not disturb
is the sign written
on a dark sky.
I bury my face
in his neck &
become silent & cool
as the night -- spent
like a passing storm.

Love In Four Fours

Lately stars seem to wink at me
over the moon's nightly appearance
voiding every pain felt in the
enabling of a different life.

Loose are my thoughts floating
obliquely from a mind
varying in depth & emotion
ever exiting and entering my psyche.

Laden are the pictures played
on my forehead as I visualize you
vicariously touching me with thought
eagerly sensed by your Lady my love.

Lost are the years of sorrow &
onward visions of fulfillment
vie for my attention & scrutiny
even as the twilight of my years race on.

Shirley's Cat House

She picked me up by car avoiding
blustery autumn winds for a ride
to her house just three short blocks
away. Shirley guided me to her
backyard where a garden tenderly
tilled still bore blossoms which
defied the weather. The tall wooden
fence suggested it was built by
a private person. I first sat on a
marble bench marveling at the beauty
of the yard decorated with hanging
bird feeders providing food to local
feathered friends. Little gardens
were strategically placed by loving hands --
embraced remembrance. But on my left
a child's playhouse caught my eye & from
that moment on I was entranced
with the multiplicity of possibilities.

Next she gave me a tour of the interior
& once again I was enveloped in a cocoon
of love still lingering after all these years.
A bowl on a shelf near the door was filled
with peanuts for begging blue jays &
squirrels. The living room invited me
to lounge but there were treasures still
waiting for my eyes to feast on.
I followed Shirley to a room where
teddy bears were neatly piled as if
waiting for a child to hug them.
Near the window was a desk I knew
belonged to Shirley's mate when he was
here on blessed Earth. Now it was hers

on which she lovingly wrote notes
to friends & family. Her bedroom
was a charming place facing gardens
enclosed with cedar fencing.
A multitude of lovely winged
creatures twirped melodies as lullabies
for a restful respite. Her blooms posed
hardy stances against the autumn
winds & there stood that lovely
playhouse which had drawn my fancy
with its potentialities.

She hosted me with coffee/tuna salad
buns & goodies in the kitchen
by a window sill full of figurines
which Shirley's daughter continued
to add to the ceramic cat cumulation.
Then I remembered the nickname
her husband gave the playhouse.
He had bought it as a gift for Shirley
to display her feline statuettes.
It was Shirley's Cat House.
Now I understood the double entendre.
I chuckled softly as she slowly
drove me home. When I later took a nap
I fantasized -- furnishing the playhouse
with a chaise a footstool & a desk
to lay my laptop. I dreamed it was
a tiny nook to call my own where
I could write or dream or meditate
at will -- a space where magic reigned
& love flowed naturally to & from
this place called Shirley's Cat House.

My Taxes Waxes

He: My back cracks as I sit to prepare
my Federal Income Tax. Let me
see? 1040 long form should work.
Well maybe not. From the booklet
I learn we have over 400 new tax
laws this year. Thank you
Congressmen & Mr. President.
Nice work!

She: I am a monumental Duh
where numbers are concerned.
I know I burn many hours
sorting receipts/canceled checks
& invoices. A shoe box here & a
plastic bag over there. I know
how much came in & where it
went but the taxable numbers are
eluding me.

He: I have piles of paper everywhere
1099s on chairs/on floor/on stairs.
The stool holds mounds of K-1
forms which presents a touchy
testy task. Piles of medical
receipts spread on carpet & I see
the cost of four operations at great
expense. Makes sense. It was
not my best year I hear but I'm
still here to pay my taxes.
According to instructions it looks
like Schedule A is for itemized
deductions. Might as well get
started.

She: Soon I will call my accountant & give
him my usual mish-mash created for
his unraveling of my illogicallities.
He earns every dollar for the trial of
translating my convoluted numbers
& deductions. So I should worry?

He: Now where's that W-2 form? Gross
income & taxes withheld &
something called FICA for when I
grow old. I'm told. Just look -- now
my calculator died. I wonder if that's
a medical expense? Could be if I lied.
Better not. Let's see. Charitable
donations first summation on
Schedule 8263. You mean to say
there are 8,262 more of these? Let's
start on Line 42. Then subtract from
Line 39 & if greater than line 41 then
enter on Schedule A -- Line 6. Oh
rats! Where's my eraser? That
should have been Line 9. Geez my
two favorite numbers.

She: I know I will get money back.
Had surgery last year.
It is intriguing to surmise the
surprise I will feel to see a check in
the mail from my beloved
government.

He: What's next? Oh taxes! Personal
property taxes/ state taxes/ car taxes
sales taxes/ capital gains taxes
interest income taxes & even taxes
on taxes. Did I miss any? I think not.

Oh bummer! I spilled coffee all over.
Quick with paper towels blot
carefully. Nope too late. It's ruined!
Transfer to new Schedule D. It's 2
AM & my eyes burn like hot coals.
So is this living or just giving?

She: I read & watch you write about
instructions & the lines just waiting
for your totals. I am baffled by your
expertise admiring all the while --
your style.

He: What's left? Oh yes. A few job
related deductions & investment
expenses for brokers' fees. I'm going
to fire that bum. Enron? You lying
sack. Nearly finished. Bring all
subtotals forward to page 2 of Form
1040. Subtract deductions from gross
income & enter on 37. Subtract
personal exemptions. Wow! Married
people should get divorced file
separately & save money. Taxable
income compare with Table A & enter
taxes owed & then subtract taxes
paid. Enter amount on Line 64.
Eureka! I paid too much & have a
refund coming. Sure as anything my
return will automatically tumble
with great gravity into the audit bin.
Just wait & see. Damn bureaucrats
anyway.

She: My taxes waxes.

Consider This

Nighttime
Insomnia
Fears
Remembrances
Ohmmmmmm
Meditating
Transformation
Phlegmatic
Analytic
Composed
Parity
Attained
Becalmed
Asleep

*Sleep state is imagined
as you travel faster
than the speed of light
& gently land
on Jupiter's 39th
satellite moon.*

*It is as well
that you don't remember
these nightly trips
because you have
pierced the veil
of your reality.*

Ohmmmmmm.

**We Are One of Many
Who Are Part of One.**

Again -- I dream
of space. That place
which holds the Whole
into a swirling
Cosmic Dance of Life.

Behold absorption
lines clue me into
secret realms --
of chemical compositions
that cloud my sleeping mind.

Time encapsulates
the Now by merging past
the present & the future
where I live while occupied
with sleep.

At times I find myself
responding to a force
whose strength attracts
my ordinary matter --
a Baryonic romance so to speak

while strong nuclear forces
pull my mass into
an unknown familiar place
where I once was a part
of something else

but always relative
to the Whole. We are
like a Binary Star --
bound & locked together not
by choice but by gravitation.

& so I ask the gods -- has the
state in which I lived before
determined where I live today
& what has caused me to
become the person I am now.

& oh the fascination of it all --
those quantum theories
of the color force which bind
those quarks together
to form protons or a spark

of sensual persuasion. I travel
in my dreams to clusters of
galaxies where I observe
the unimaginable. It is here I find
where I belong for all is too familiar.

I dream . . . .

Remembering Tomorrow

Curtains sway in Autumn's breeze.
A hint of burning leaves wafts
through our windows. Harvest
moon's glow silhouettes ripe
shapeliness as her twinkling eyes
dance with devilish mischief &
play begins with tickles & giggles.
Lips brush -- noses rub like
Eskimos as arms enfold into
embrace of renewed promises.

Supple breasts press taut to
my chest & I smooth from her
radiant face -- raven hair filled
with scent of morning flowers.
Rapacious mouths feed
voraciously as limbs entwine like
clinging vines & fever burns with
enraptured anticipation. Hunger
grows deep within like raging
wild fires sweeping through forests.

Searching hands explore once
again & ears listen for familiar
signals -- a small gasp/moan
whispered words or a playful
nibble. Her thigh rises unfolding
flower petals moist with love's elixir.
Guided with purpose I'm bathed
in her sweet nectar. Pace is a slow
pleasurable give & receive --
then suddenly a tiny gasp summons.

Her strength commands &
I eagerly surrender control
as backs arch & hips strike
a rhythm fundamental to
the soul. Moisture appears
like morning dew on her
upper lip & her eyes now
lidded. My ears roar like a
train in a tunnel as we reach
coherent heights. Rabid

throes & muffled shrieks
intensify as she trembles
& bites the pillow.
Zealous thighs exert her will
as I'm drawn into a demanding
clutch -- pulsing. Sounds of
beating jungle drums pierce my
mind & white light flashes --
blinding. Our crescendo peaks
as she peals & trembles & I howl --

shuddering. We clutch tight &
seize the moment for minutes --
absorbing. We collapse filled
with bliss as tender stroking
& light kisses reaffirm our deep
commitment. Cuddling like
matching spoons we float away
to paradise on white puffy clouds.
Look! You can see us
against the Harvest moon.

Time & Change.

The Role of Repetition

So be it!

Moon goes through its phases
masking one side we do not see
& though I cannot visually grasp
that point of view which always hides
its features from an earth possessed
I am afflicted with the sickness
of a human being who's lost control
finding herself dominated by Moon
Moon,
      Moon,
            Moon!

Calendared Menses are dictated by
Moon & wolves howl at Moon.
Even I howl at Moon in fixated adoration
& sense the slow slithering of a veiled
Sun's heat penetrate my skin -- my eye/I.
It is then I feel alive with ancient rhythms
coaxing my being into *Being* & I hear the
drums and beats of a heart pound
insistently in every conscious cell -- every
circulating drop of blood by the pull
& power traveling through frigid space by
Moon,
      Moon,
            Moon!

Finally I've found the one who can truly
dominate & force me to scan the sky
to see its glow -- the subtle change in tone
& its varied geometricals in awe. So be it!

The Night Has Been A Carrier

Absence of Light
blocks vision.
Roses lack color
& insects are mute.
Night's beauty
is scarred -- marred
by emptiness
& all has been stilled
by Fate's inconstancy.
Night birds are songless
mourning moon's *in absentia.*
Earth is blanketed
by a dense smog
caused by poisons emitted
& acid tears add blindness
in this night
of a sleeping Light.
Afternoons may bring
surcease from sorrow
but Night suggests magic
for someone like me.
I cry -- skin burns
sizzles on cheeks
felt but not seen.
I exist
on the dark side
of the Moon.

A Vulnerable State Indeed

Indians/ghosts
whispering winds
in the trees -- spirits
moving in the room.
The moon sweeps
a path of shadows
across two lovers
shaped like elongated
stars or the phallus
of an ancient mariner
traversing the Heavens.
They are entwined like
vines in celestial vineyards.
These phantom lovers
insinuate silhouettes
on lids fluttering madly.
Their images dance within
rapid eye movements
announcing a REM state
of shallow sleep.
The Dream Weaver
saturates the senses
in our most vulnerable
state. We cannot move
& if we do it is
the movement governed
by the Astral Body seeking
escape from the physical.
Ahhh we dream --
of fleeing & floating
away from
the bonds of gravity.

With & Without

Life without dreams
a hollow existence
suspended in Time
& Space --
a continuum of twilight.
Absent high energy
sunfilled days &
star filled nights for
Dreamers.
An emptiness echoes
unfulfilled goals --
broken plans excise
self worth & deposit
bitter biting pain
as loneliness grows.

Escape to another world
in mind & matter brings
mollification to broken
hearts healing. In
this world of happiness --
hot sun shining
days for plans &
contemplation
& scintillating stars
to wish upon.
Appetites grow as
high energy copiously
abounds -- grand plans
ascribed -- faces smile
while wishes come true
& dreams are real.
Happiness -- Dream on.

A Train Whistles At The Junction

A train whistles at the junction
stirring familiar recollections.
Imagination calls to a soul
dreaming of escape & change.
Sounds differentiate trains
& some whistles can pierce
the deepest sleep. We hear it
wailing far away & dreamers
ride the dream with engine
chug-chugging on their
subconsciousness.

Train station scurrying
provides backdrop while
two travelers greet each other
with familiarity though
they have never met before.
A station full of passengers
& greeters do not distract
the couple bound beyond
boundaries. They meet --
shake hands sedately. It is
a script which has been
written in pulses pleading
for an audience of two.

Curtains are drawn
against the day & privacy
is a blanket protecting
them against querying
onlookers at stations waiting
for their own fantasy. They
embrace -- clutch the rhythm

of the train's movements
& blush at pleasure
shared while paired.
Comfort carries them along
in each other's caresses
& the scent of love mingles
with the air. Precious Time
races for these two lovers.
The call to travel has
become an urgency --
to feel miles disappear
through curtained window
once again. We've all been on
that train. A sleek transporter
of yearnings where images
visualized are wheeled to us
for real. Time has traveled on
& like the train it too has
a destination. Lovers
meanwhile share the wails
of loneliness as the train
whistles at the junction of despair.

Every Time Is Now
(The Past, Present & Future)

There is a pause --
a necessary reflection
on the effects of Time.
It moves in many directions
the present -- future
& the past where guidelines
are required unless one is a
practiced space traveler
knowing changes are constant --
exist incrementally in Time
in what has happened --
is happening & what will happen.

I follow my heart -- compelled
for I am disarmed & helpless
riding each moment's wave --
aware of an awesome power
which dictates my transitions.

The Past.

I am a creature by design
for a double helical
predestines my physical
& mental structure.
One with genes which pattern
behavioral traits
& develops my soul.
A babe caught in the swirl & twirl
of a chaotic Universe I am a part of
but cannot comprehend.
I fight/grow & survive

yet I am aware of the probabilities
that all my energies can do
to postpone the inevitable
bonding with another *being* who
may divert my destination. I am
adaptable -- an evolver -- a survivor.

Analysis says all is sameness
because of grand scheme's replication.
This past is one I followed
like puppy after its master
not knowing the consequences
of behavior. It then became clear
& understood that *I* alone
predicted my future
which is now my present.

The Present.

The present
is like a train barely moving.
I am in *limbo* without direction --
suspended between two time zones
a committed soul cued for passage.
It's like waiting for Godot.
Time remits as I face
mortality's ace-in-the-hole.
Nevertheless
frameworks form fancies
of rainbow's glistening promise.
This nexus enervates.
Angel's blessings beckon me.
I know. I still wait for the train
to move me into the future.

The Future.

So here I am --
connecting visually
meditatively & virtually.
These emotions carry promise.
My treasure chest
at the end of that rainbow
awaits key in hand.
Time vacillates --
swaying back & forth.

Looking back I understand
the crush of dashed plans --
lingering disappointments.
Time wasn't ready to move
but now the train
has arrived at the future.
Wisdom grew & knew
the when & why of it all.
I smell rain/snow/dew
hear rivers flow --
greeting me
each morning of my life.
I now know how wind
shakes trees
& grows ocean waves
traveling to known destinations.
I am here. Now. In the future
of my reveries.

¿Que Cosa Esta Noche?
(What is This Thing – This Night?)

---

and why am I here

across from you -- a stranger I see
who walks on air as I amongst the trees?
& why do I lay a light kiss upon your cheek --
tell you stories of my fiery indiscretions
from a past which never leaves my memory.
It is a recollection which chains & claims
those alpha states where all is possible

like now

finding myself above the backyard tree
eyes level with the nested birds who peek
while Moon plays me like an errant love
bloating up to full for my repast.

I've flown across the tracks before
& hovered over this old tree -- my gown
a'blowin' in the wind of dreams
while levitating in between two worlds.
One with your face facing me across
the branches of a timed response & the other
watching myself travel as a wraith with
white gown flowing 'round my nebulous flesh
glowing radiantly as if speckled by silver
moonbeams as I slowly sank in the folds
of my familiar fantasy. My bed floats.
Or is this too my fancy dredged from the dirt
of old plots & old romances turned to dust?

Now You See It. Now You Don't.

Imagine early December rain
turning into snow while you slept
for just an hour -- flakes falling
larger than Kennedy half-dollars.
Then imagine streets & lawns
covered with white cotton until
all dirt & disarray disappear.
You watch the birds you feed
each day search for food beneath
this chilly blanket. You put on
a robe to get more seed from
the garage -- sprinkle it upon
familiar paths. After feeder has
been filled & ground areas covered
you watch from a window with
wonderment as the scene is
speckled in hues of blues/reds
browns against a snowy coverlet.
Two cardinals battle as do
the bluejays/squirrels & grackles
but none will be forced from their
place at the table.

You lie down once more sleeping
with a smile on your face. Two
hours more elapse & you wake up --
look outside see snow has changed
to rain & reality. Now all dirt &
disarray reappears. You rub eyes
& wonder was it just a dream --
dreamt in white?

Ten Hours of Sleep

in which I disappeared into a life not lived
in a time frame I controlled. Here in an
undetermined space speed was instantaneous
& past was now the present. Future flickerings
of place demanded tortuous tribulations & need
was labeled a distraction. I watched two high
energy particles obliterate each other with
panache & I felt the pricks of pain protest.

Head holds many surprises & brain plays mind
(or vice versa) with capabilities of unknowns.
How many planets did I visit & how many
aliens did I love? Or does it really make a
difference? In dreams all *IS* & thusly approved.
For how can I undo what has been done unless I
ride the speed train to the past? & in most
circumstances I cannot recall what *IS* & less
what *WAS*. An excellent arrangement made
by memory.

So I will wipe the sleep of hours from my eyes
and shake my head at driblets dribbling by with
snippets of the life I lived in sleep induced
by body needs. I will profess to all rejuvenation
of my sensuality by demons seeking to possess
what always has been theirs & I will smile at
them & feign subservience while stripping all
those little devils in my cells of strength.
In dreams nothing is impossible. I am a
testament to tacit transmutations.

Resonance

He: My voice pealed through her. Every frequency caused a shudder throughout the spectrum. It was resonance.

She: And I trembled like a leaf blown by the wind -- wondering all the while at the lightness of *being*.

(The Unconscious speaks in wet whispers slurring speech patterns purring pussycat phrases into the ears of the one who listens with tongue in cheek.)

She: Your lips are so soft & insistent. Your tongue snakes in me like it found a home.

(I see a canvas of black space occupied with what is there but cannot be perceived. I am enclosed in a private place of unencumbered allusions & I fight the force to no avail. I am cocooned in a gravitational pull & there I stay -- waiting for space to do its will.)

He: She has become mine. I hold her with Love & the Universe I offer dances in my eyes as I see her wait for me in a space without color. I shall bring her Light & Life as she resonates with our familiar frequencies.

She: I wait.

The Waiting & Twisting Of Time

I've seen Time pause
while minutes snailed
its slow persistent path.
Clocks stalled
anticipation by
backward glances
at hackneyed hands
which refused
lineal predispositions.

I've seen Time twist
by the effects of bent
control clutching motion
in its grip. It is then when
memories march
backwards tense-wise
ripping apart illusions
of chronology & one is left
reliving a persecutory past.

I've seen Time speed forward
whooshing velocity's desire
to end delicious moments.
Apparent prisoners of Time
are we -- waiting & counting
man-made minutes into hours
only to experience a warped
loss of reception which
cannot be controlled.

The Visitors

We experiment with the mind --
multiplexing transmission
of brain power through concentration.
Mutuality you say!
I lie in bed with palms upward
to accept the Light --
let it enter me & hence begins
the Visualization.
I am a floating aura
merging with the metal chair
& your bed. Behold the box
hovering over you! Observe it spread
its contents of miniature stars
through your brain & body.
Feel the pressure points
on your afflicted areas
& feel the healing tingle.

The healings help
& aware technicians
are witness to rapid eye movements
gone berserk. They've been informed
of your experimentations.
You are focused & see
my shapeless form of Light
with upward palms.

My floating aura has drifted
from the metal chair
& hovers over you
to enter your being until we are one.
I see your organs
from an internal vantage

& marvel at the human machine.
Our hands reach to touch
& they spark for fractions of Time.
Infectious Viruses are slowly dying
from the Light.

Those Viruses are almost gone
my dear. Those medications
were effective & the help of mutual
Visualization also was a healing tool.
You have seen me dance
over your form with my aura --
enter your afflicted areas.
You have felt billions
of miniature stars enter your brain
& body -- the pressure points
of intrusion. It has been
a mutual affair of mind/belief
& love. My upward palms
are now clenched fists of Faith.

We have traveled mentally
through concentration. Now
we watch our astral journey end
with selves at rest.

The Question is About Time

Night has descended.
A dark curtain
obscures light.
Yet mind *sees* scenes
which disturb
the waves of sleep --
birthing nightmares.
What time is it
here on Earth
& is it really relevant
in the Universe?
What time is it there --
where Bubble Universes
dwell at the edge
of Elsewhere?

Will Time allow you
to hold me once again
& will it be as heavenly
on Earth as it is
in the Universe?
I question Time
time & time again
but no response
except the ticking
away of my life.

Only Time Will Be Allowed To Dictate

Yes-s-s-s-s-s-s-s-s-s-s-s
disport my empty hours
with proportionality.
Let me journey through
life with Time on my side.
Kiss-s-s-s-s-s-s-s-s-s-s
family & friends good-bye
when Time demands it.
The last breath is always
the hardest fought for.

I've been absent from myself
since I have met *Obsession.*
The shadow dressed in mourning
speaks loudly for this occasion
& eyes which sparkled once
with Life have dimmed
to an illusion of existence
on this planet we call Earth.
Love can be a killer of vitality
so I see my coffin slowly being made.

So disport my empty hours
with proportionality.
Let me kiss my friends & family
while Time allows me to consider.
I've been absent from myself
since I have met *Obsession.*
I've become a shadow dressed
in black dimmed to an illusion.
I'm being slowly killed by Love
or lack of same on planet Earth.

Tomorrow Is Long Coming

Fall is encroaching slowly
twisting temperatures --
reflecting capriciousness
of weather systems.
Summer heat lingers
loathe to leave for the other
hemisphere. Creeping cool
evenings demand subtle
wardrobe changes. I wrap
sweaters & light jackets
around my body seeking
warmth from the wind plus
addition of that extra blanket
on the bed. Air is moist with
warnings of approaching
storms as our dog lies near
my feet protected from
elemental furies. Deciduous
leaves tinged with Autumn's
spectra gather against walls
& fences -- gossiping gusts
before the storm. Dust devil
dervishes rise in vortices
then quickly disappear into
nothingness waiting for change
in the next incarnation.
A clap of thunder -- the first
splat of rain strikes powdered
dust leaves' imprint then
is quickly smothered.

The storm is here!

Clogged gutters soon fill
& overflow from drenching
downpours. Sun-baked Earth
sips with delicacy as excesses
flood small streams & valleys.
Weather Seers proclaim that
niños/niñas have moderated
& our jet stream sweeps
southward in a cold arctic dance
for Winter. Dreams insist
on being dreams of the future
& I meditate -- visualizing
what has not happened
in the *Now*. Tomorrow is
an image of fulfillment not yet
realized. Today is wrought
with apprehensions of decisions
made. Faith is the cane I lean on.
I must not fall before tomorrow.
For it all will come to pass
when tomorrow becomes today.

Where Does Time Go?

I have this old watch which ticks
out loudly proud to be heard
despite my distractions.

I am aware of *Time* because of this
incessant ticking on my wrist
which tweaks remembrances.

It must be sleep or meditation deep
which slows the processes
of knowing or of joy while

living in the present urging Time
to still itself but yet where does it go
this skipping of awareness

when simultaneously those hours
at some moments crawled in mind?
Yet all the while I smile

at the results at end of day because
it sped at speeds without a pause.
Time races to unknown destinations

elusive like a lie perceived --
misunderstanding while it ticks on
at its own pace to a place

      forever changing.

Disconnected

Too slow to catch
a thought.
Been sleeping
too much.

I speak in short
statements.
Too lazy for
long sentences.

Brewing tempers
terrorize me.
Veiled constructs
hold me together.

Emotional
thermostat is set
to high. Might
internally combust.

House echoes
silence.
Phone is
ringless.

Fingers are
separate.
I watch
them type.

Fascinating.

Briar's Crossing

Florescent hues of oranges & yellows
from sugar maples scintillate
as Autumn creeps in like playful puppies.
Sweater weather approaches
& hot apple cider memories grow vivid
as tongue tastes Winesap juices.
Night's frost lingers in shadows --
sparkling diamonds in morning's crisp
dawn. Maple seeds swirl like landing
helicopters as gray bushy-tailed squirrels

scamper gathering Autumn's bounties.
Surrounding hills -- carpeted with
leaves of golden sycamores -- glowing
yellow poplars & shimmering orange
sugar maple trees transfix *Time.*
Smoke trails from red brick chimneys
as Briar's Crossing awakes this brisk
Autumn morning. A covered bridge
spans Briar's Creek white water rapids
floating rainbow colored leaves like

a moving efflorescent garden.
The scent of burning leaves wafts
through the Crossing & fresh maple
syrup heats on the stove. A flock
of Canada geese fly south for wintering
in the Chesapeake. Sleek black &
gray birds of migration follow their
leader in Vee formation like he has
the only compass. Familiar honks echo
through Briar's Crossing as if to say
See You In Springtime.

Return To The

World Of Wet

Soundings

Sounding depths is like
fathoming the mind.
Sunken histories haunt
endlessly. Obscurities
vanish when surfaced.
Ambient noises interfere
with measurements
seeking brain signals.

Waves of thought distort
images lurking underneath
the pings of repetitious rates.[1]
Delving depths can be
deceiving. Dark shadows
threaten -- clear echoes ring
precision. Reaching bottom --
probing sources of actions
must be done with a steady
hand holding the line.

Tedious testing may become
a constant depending upon
consistency. Varying
pressures regulate pace of
comprehension. Shallows can
be dangerous. Light dependent
hues have misleading
qualities not to be trusted.

*1. Pulse Repetition Rate: The times per minute a SONAR or
Fathometer sends out pulses, called "pings"*

Yesterday
(Dedicated to September 11, 2001)

---

you thought tomorrow would
bring light --
those quiet shadowed footfalls
could cease following

today is almost gone
you can feel the tension
grinding through your teeth
& taste the iron on your tongue

while yesterday's smoke lingers --
choking lungs & tearing eyes
today's smoldering passions ignite
& pieces coalesce a oneness

as the planet Earth rotates
on its axis of despair & in its
orbit of deception -- just look
at yonder darkening horizon

global storm clouds gathering
hemispherical lightning strikes as rains
of terror tumble from skies -- I pray
there is no tomorrow like yesterday

Impedimenta

Mind scurries
worries
plays hide & seek.
Sitting still --
unsure of maps
staring --
daring me to return
on the road to life.

Don't drive anymore.
Traffic intimidates.
Don't fly anymore.
Terrorists intrepidate!
Dependence on others
to reach destinations
has grounded me.

Attempt to grasp a dream
so far away but speed
leaves a red-shift & me
behind. Even directions
are misguiding. All
beguiling roads come
back to beginnings
leaving me farther away.

Eyes no longer see
leaving me lost
in unknowing darkness
traveling by touch
amongst the mazes.

Daffy

I wait for Spring --
been hibernating during
freezing Winter months
in a dark dry box
in the cellar. I sense
sun's radiant warmth
seep through window
curtains & begin
to awaken. Tender hands
lovingly remove me
from my gloomy enclosure
taking me to the light.

Soon I will once again
be pampered -- gently
patted into soft mulched
soil to propagate. Now
sun smiles upon me
& Spring's ritual begins --
absorbing moisture &
preparations to generate
roots for feeding.

My white sprouts
appear to be reaching
for sun's energy
growing upward towards
air to begin the process
of photosynthesis & turn
a rich emerald green.

I break soil's surface & observe
a red breasted bird pulling
worms from flower bed while
being praised by his mate
sitting a nearby nest.

A stem has suddenly shot from
my bulb & is developing a bud
on the tip. As I look at my
neighbors -- I see happy yellow
faces. Maybe my face will
bloom a smile tomorrow.

A tiny bird with wings so fast
I cannot see -- drinks deeply
of my nectar. I watch a lady
with brimmed hat cut stems
& place flowery faces
in her basket. I smell her
fragrance as she passes by --
I wonder if she smells
mine. It is Summer -- & scent
blows with the sultry breeze.

In hot Summer sun
my face browns & withers
away leaving leaves to stay
to feed me. I notice days
are growing shorter & there
is a chill in the air. It is late
Fall. I'm being dug up & look!
I have multiplied!
I am three bulbs now.

We will *be* again
in the Spring.

Lights! Camera! Enter Spring!

Dark Winter's thoughts
fade as weather warms --
of past withering plants
of dead blossoms on the vine
& leaves crackling under
trampling boots. So know
ye all who think of death --
that is but a cycle of *change*
& Spring is here at last
to prove me right.

Sprouts push their stems
through Earth like green
arrows seeking sun.
They bud before your eyes
just as the years grant
you life. Flowers bare
their faces shamelessly --
nature's coloring
providing cosmetic
foundations. Diversity
flourishes everywhere.
Complexions vibrate
to the sun -- quiver with life
& sensuality.

Crazed by scent & juices
insects fly/crawl/buzz around
these rouged harlots.
The dance of life continues
& love is rekindled
beneath a beneficent
Spring full moon.

Pineapple Express*

1.

Silence enraptures my being. I sense
my body functions doing their duty --
enjoying being alive as I do. Heavy
wet snow falling for hours piles deep
clinging to evergreen boughs bending
low. Wind whispers -- absent. Skies
weighted with dark clouds. Nothing
moves. A warming trend promised
meteorology sages -- tardy like young
boys for school. A whimsical dream
transports me beyond somewhere to
someone somehow. Time passes
unmetered. Nothing stirs -- only feelings.

2.

Three days prior arctic zephyrs warned
snow was coming. I sensed/smelled &
felt it in my bones. Clear cold nights
well below freezing. Cold front began
to weaken & moved eastward as strong
winds battered western coastlines. Pineapple
Express* brought water saturated clouds

* *Pineapple Express: A subtropical central north Pacific
Ocean low pressure weather cell which forms southwest of
Hawaii and travels rapidly in a northeasterly direction
towards the continent carrying warm moist air in a
conveyer belt fashion by high winds aloft. This heavily
laden moist air condenses into rain as it travels into cooler
air masses of northern latitudes producing heavy warm
rain from Los Angeles in the south to British Columbia,
Canada in the north.*

from Hawaiian seas. Cold & wet
converged over Puget Sound
& volcanic born Olympic Mountains
gathered white comforter around head
& shoulders. Soon foothills gentle slopes
& valleys followed accumulated white
quilts & plump pillows. In doldrums
I waited as the first breath moved from
southwest & delivered promised
warming light rain.

Now one soft drip from an eve joins
my reverie. Soon many more follow
& sounds of melting snow run in gutters
all around. My focus sharpens senses
acute. My heart warms to new thoughts
as water begins to flow. I share with my
online partner delicate sounds of melting
snow-drips as they grow in linear
transformation. Volume now rushes
downspouts ever louder. The thaw is here!
I step outside undercover of deck roof
observe gathering trickles on the hillside
listen to storm drains rush-gush
flowing faster to harbor release. Rain
filled snow -- heavy hanging -- drops from
evergreen tree/boughs & dwellings.
Limbs snap/snow splats splashes
melting faster. Trickles growing
into streams flowing toward rivers
surging toward the sea to repeat
the cycle. I see crocus peeking
through melting snow. My face
smiles a welcome -- hearty friend.
We weather weather together
& shall survive.

Drowning In My Dreams

I meditate --
visualizing my aquarium
in slow motion. Colors
bright flow through
my mind & a figurine
diver expels rising bubbles.

My mind
becomes a lake clear
as non-thought. Living
room shimmers as I float
on my back like an otter
body bobbing on lazy
waves lapping the walls.
The shore of my living
room disappears as all
walls slowly fade away
like unwanted distractions
sinking below my horizon.
This meditative state
grows deeper & I am
swept away by larger
waves of imagination
set free from restraint.
The lake becomes
a swollen thought
expanding into
illogical logicality.

My Dream Lake
teems with giant tropical
fish. Each one a hundred
fold larger than they were

in their home aquarium
habitat. My mind has
expanded & I am
astonished at images
confronting me. A school
of nine neon tetras nibble
about my knees like
greeting a stranger new
to the neighborhood.
Bright iridescent blues
& reds saturate my color
comprehension. They
slowly move away as
I stare at guppies the size
of bread loaves. Six
in number pass with
barely a blink of recognition
as if on a mission to the far
side of nowhere. I recoil
defensively from two bright
orange swordtails much
larger than me. They bump
my shoulder & thigh as if
to sample the menu then
move in search of another
source for food. I relax --
regaining composure
as I gaze in wonderment
& appreciate the spectacle
of three silver blackstriped
angel fish the size of canine
animals passing the floating
upside down couch in what
was once my living room.
My sense of safety from
predators is short lived

as a red-tailed shark
twice my size slowly waves
his tail keeping stationary
as if calculating where to
strike for the most tasty
morsel. Nearly frozen
in fear I gently tread water --
eyes fixed on eyes for an
equivocal eternity when
suddenly -- sleek as a seal
swimming swiftly the now
man-sized frogman drives
my nemesis away.

My recliner floats past
& I grab a hold on
the opened foot rest. I climb
up & sit on the recliner
riding the lake in comfort
& safety knowing Archimedes[1]
would hold.

I see my doggie paddling
towards me head held high
all legs motoring like she
was chasing a cat. I help her
aboard my recliner. She
shakes violently spraying
indiscriminately. I hold
my arms up for protection
then realize there is no need --
the deed is done.

1: *Archimedes' Principle: A body floating or submerged in
a liquid is buoyed up by a force equal to the weight of the
liquid displaced.*

I see slick magazines
slowly become saturated
& find their way to
the floor. Three sofa
cushions rise to
the surface like
bubbling bubbles
in a lava lamp.
My dining table
looks like a landing
platform for tiny
planes & a lampshade
bobs to the surface
without the lamp
like a blind lighthouse
on a distant shore.

Clutter from my home
office now floats
about me -- a letter
here an invoice there
looking for their inbox
with despair. Books
from shelves are freed
for new eyes to consume
& ponder the inscrutable.
I reach for a favorite
but my ride has moved.
I cannot reach it
& I fear my book will
drown & maybe me.

My clothes are wet.
Sun sinks
at an alarming rate.
It's getting cold & I cower

from the coming darkness --
fear of unknown bumps
or touches of the night
& my imagination.

I suddenly wake up
my arms flailing in fear
my doggie whining
her concern as the TV
movie ends --
all survivors in lifeboats
as their ship slips
beneath my carpet
sinking in my living room
lake of dreams.

Rain Forest

Gentle rain falls & light wind-wisps whirl
wetted shadows like fading ballerinas
as a darkened sky creeps ashore on Pointe'
shoes[1] Daily drenching temperate climes
perpetuate this virgin primal evergreen
wonderment. Majestic conifers -- Sitka
spruce/Douglas fir & red cedar stand
sentinel for centuries.

Wind ruffles regal trees -- soft sounds
emanate whisper/murmur/moan & creak.
Boughs bend low -- drip/drop/drip -- on
saturated mosses/lichens/fungi & parasitics
alike. Life proliferates atop/within & under
the canopy. Ground is strewn like children's
pickup sticks decades deep -- decomposing
trees/needles/foliage & conifer cones.
A Pileated[2] woodpecker's relentless tattoo
shatters woodland's reverie as tiny
bunnies five in number pause -- listen --
& then resume nibbling tender berry shoots --
their black noses rhythmic bouncing like
diminutive balls.

Bright green moss carpets forest floors
& grows on weathered trees fallen &

[1]: shoes: Pointe' shoes: Ballet shoes with wooden blocks in
the toes for toe dancing, from the French, Sur les pointe',
also known as point work.
[2]: Pileated: Pileated woodpecker: crow size, 17 inches in
height, black and white striped neck, white under-wings
lining, prominent red crest, male has red mustache, female
has black, eats carpenter ants in fallen and/or dead timber.

standing & all organic decay cycles
sustenance. Nearly tropical is the
luxuriance with undergrowth of vine
maples/rhododendron & big leaf maples.
Ferns grow four stories tall like a lacy green
temple reaching for dappled sunlight their
roots feeding on natural nutrients & bathed
in twelve feet of rainfall each year. A nurse[3]
tree fallen many years before gradually
fades away as it provides life to seven
young cedars stretching tall into canopy.
Ring-tailed raccoons -- black masked faces sip
from stream then scamper like toddlers
snitching from a cookie jar up an old
growth spruce for lazy napping.

Gathering pools foster tiny tinkling trickles
sparkling water gravity tugged to crystal
cantillating streams to river's stentorian
dissonance of white water's path to Mother
Ocean -- another cycle completed.

Ivy vines hang long & sway gently in the
soddened breeze -- beckon attention
to red-brown pine squirrels racing along slender
boughs high overhead performing death defying
acrobatics like circus trapeze performers
as they deftly leap from one tree to another.

Birds fill the trees & serenade welcoming songs
to the Olympic Rain Forest[4.] Behold
the Hall of Mosses -- grand greens all hues
stand tall -- a wide hall ceremoniously created
over ages holding to trees/bushes & saplings
alike. A magnificent emerald glow of Paradise.

3. *Nurse tree: conifer (evergreen cedar, fir pine and spruce) trees fallen to the ground and through the decaying process provides nutrients (nurse) to sprouts from seeds and/or parts of the fallen tree that takes root in and through the dying host tree trunk, sending new trees up from and down through, establishing roots in the ground, the fallen tree. As many as nine new trees are known to be growing from one nurse tree in The Olympic Rain Forest.*

4: *Olympic Rain Forest: located in the western foothills of Olympic National Park, established in 1938. The park encompasses most of the home of the Olympic Mountains, from the Pacific Ocean on the West, to Hood's Canal on the East, forming the Olympic Peninsula. The forest is one of the finest remaining areas of virgin rain forest in the Pacific northwest, in particular, and the world, in general. Annual precipitation is among the heaviest in the United States, where rainfall averages about 144 inches per year. The significance of this particular temperate climate rain forest is that the forest has never been logged/harvested for wood products at all. What exists now, looks nearly the same as the rain forest did thousands of years ago. A continuous cycling process exists today as it has for centuries and with our tender consideration will continue far into the future.*

I Would Never Run
(Except Towards You)

Those letters
swim before me.
I cannot move
my eyes from ripples
caused by their
arrangements.

Water washes
over words
splashing its
fragrances of salt &
death & life struggling
in the dance.

Waves crash
against my bosom --
those crests reaching
for my lips & I lie
transfixed at this mobility
lusting to fuse
with its counterpart.

I'm brought to shore by
senses. Laid on the sand
shifting beneath my wet
body & there above me is
a shadow bending over me
breathing his life
into my waiting lungs.

I live!

Seeds

So here I am watching --
waiting for a seed
to manifest its destiny.
Day after day I look
for thrust of stem
to penetrate earth's surface.
Nothing!
It rains. Lightning cracks!
Thunder roars power
from the Heavens & I seek
refuge in my sleep
curled up like an embryo
in a mother's womb.

A start in a dream awakens me
& I throb because I *know*
something special has occurred
in my sleep while the rains came.

Dawn is a dismal affair
but I open my door with expectancy.
Ah yes! There it is.
Stem's protrusion.
Seed has established its will
amongst the grasses.

Tomorrow I shall plant
another seed & anticipate
its germination. Tonight
I sleep to dream wondering
if the rains will bring me once again
a fiery storm of pleasure.   I wait.

Biography of Dr. Edward L. Smith.

Edward L. Smith is an ocean physicist and in his sunset years returned to his native state of Washington, where he provides scientific research consulting services to The University Of Washington and others. He received his degrees in physics from San Diego State University and University of California, San Diego. He conducted, as Senior Scientist, more than fifty at-sea experiments in ocean acoustics. He has published nearly one-hundred scientific papers in various professional journals, both national and international and is the author of two books and the co-author of another on the propagation of underwater sound, and served as technical editor for a fourth. He served as a civilian scientist for the US Navy and Defense Departments in several capacities. As Director of the Defense Advanced Research Project Agency's Acoustic Research Center and the Office of Naval Research as the Director of the Long Range Acoustics Propagation Project. He has received many and various professional awards including The President's Award for Distinguished Civilian Service. He is a Fellow of the Washington (DC) Academy of Sciences, a Fellow of The Acoustical Society of America, a member of The International Geophysical Union, a member of the National Academy of Sciences, and other professional societies. Following a career in government, he owned and served as Chairman and Chief Executive Officer of B-K Dynamics, Inc., a large diversified high-technology consulting firm. He sold his consulting business in 1994, but continues to independently consult on challenging problems for interesting organizations. He serves as a Director on The Board of Directors of two well know technology corporations. As a young man, he pursued a future in music as a percussionist and performed with several well know jazz ensembles and big dance bands. He remains a patron of the arts, but his heart still lives in the jazz world. Dr. Smith began poetry writing, February 2000, with Ms Carmen M. Pursifull as his mentor. To date, he has co-authored, with Ms Pursifull, more than one-hundred poems and they have published 22 of their poems in various Anthologies. This is their first book as co-authors.

Carmen M. Pursifull was born and raised in New York City where she grew up and was educated. Her mother was Spanish and her father was Puerto Rican. She became a professional dancer and dance instructor with Joe Piro, (known as Killer Joe, because of his expertise in dancing,) at the old Palladium Ballroom on Broadway, as well as a vocalist with several well-known Latin bands during the Mambo craze of the early 1950's. She married a career US Navy man and lived in many places, including both U.S. coasts and her father's homeland of Puerto Rico. She raised a daughter and son and is a grandmother of eight and a great-grandmother of five. In 1970, following retirement from the Navy, she and her husband moved to Champaign, Illinois, to live near their son, who was attending The University Of Illinois. Four years later, following an intense period of poetry and literature study, she joined The Red Herring Poetry Workshop and began writing poems. Since then, she has published over five hundred poems and six collections of poetry: *Carmen By Moonlight* (1982); *The Twenty-Four Hour* (1989*); Manhattan Memories* (1989); *Elsewhere In A Parallel Universe* (1992); *The Many Faces of Passion* (1996) *and Brimmed Hat With Flowers, (Multitasking.com)* (2000). She is Senior Poetry Editor for Dream International Quarterly; Now, Publisher for Hawk Productions, and organizes poetry readings for The Red Herring Poets. Carmen M. Pursifull is listed on-line at the Illinois Writers Directory and The Academy of American Poets, as well as other sites. She will soon have a Homepage at R.R. Bowker on-line with her poetry partner, Edward L. Smith. Nearly three years ago, this partnership brought forth the new combined voice, demonstated in this new book, *World Of Wet.*